C000115764

JESUS WAS BORN IN ZERO BC

USING GOD'S ORIGINAL CALENDAR

CLARENCE BOYKIN JR.

Copyright © 2024 **Clarence Boykin Jr. Publishing**

All rights reserved. No part of this publication may be reproduced, distributed, or transmitted in any form or by any means, including photocopying, recording, or other electronic or mechanical methods, without the prior written permission of the publisher, except in the case of brief quotations embodied in critical reviews and certain other noncommercial uses permitted by copyright law. For permission requests, write to the publisher, addressed "Attention: Book Rights and Permission," at the address below.

Published in the United States of America

ISBN 978-1-959173-70-0 (SC)
ISBN 978-1-960684-11-0 (Ebook)

Clarence Boykin Jr. Publishing
19974 Murray Hill St.
Detroit MI 48235
Jesuswasbornzerobc@gmail.com

Ordering Information and Rights Permission:

Quantity sales. Special discounts might be available on quantity purchases by corporations, associations, and others. For details, contact the publisher at the address above.

For Book Rights Adaptation and other Rights Permission. Call us at 313.556.6145 or send us an email at Jesuswasbornzerobc@gmail.com

I dedicate this book to God, since God, through His Spirit, has revealed these revelations for the edification of His body that we all may grow in His Son Jesus Christ. Amen and Amen.

WHAT OTHERS ARE SAYING

"Clarence Boykin has accomplished what must be done if you are going to make a startling statement. He has done his research, expressed his views and opinions regarding that research, and has given the readers adequate information necessary to make a personal decision. Whether the reader agrees with him or not, the information in his book will have to be addressed."

Dr. Richard Tate, PhD

JESUS WAS BORN IN ZERO BC

USING GOD'S ORIGINAL CALENDAR

CONTENTS

INTRODUCTION

God is the Author of time! Jesus was born in zero BC was written from the end to the beginning, therefore you want find any elaborate explanations, trying to convince you into believing something that isn't true. The Holy Bible is the greatest historical book ever written to date. The scriptures were written under the inspiration of God by many men over time. The scriptures with the calendars show you the impossibilities that men could orchestrated the complexities of mending the Old Testament with the New Testament and vice versa. The scriptures are connected to God One World Calendar (GOWC) from the beginning to the end. GOWC was designed around the life of Jesus Christ. Jesus Christ was born on Sunday February/Shebeth 1, 3642 GOWC that was 3,642 years 1 month from the first day, better known as, Before Christ (BC). We are going to prove that the Old Testament to the birth of Jesus Christ are contained within those years and month. God instructed Moses to write the first five books of the Holy Bible called the Pentateuch using GOWC.

This is how GOWC begins:

> In the beginning God created the heaven and the earth. And God said, Let there be light: and there was light. And God saw the light, that it was good: and God divided the light from the darkness. And God called the light Day, and the darkness he called Night. And the evening and the morning were the first day. Sunday January 1.   Genesis 1:1-5 (emphasis added)

When you read the scriptures, you must rightly interpret them. Everything in the heaven and the earth has it beginning from God. Most people think the 24 hours day is from 12 a.m. to 12 a.m. instead of God truth, which is 6 p.m. to 6 p.m. Can man alteration change God truth? No. Even when you don't honor God truth, the truth does not change.

> And the evening and the morning were the second day. Monday January 2. Genesis 1:8 (emphasis added)

> And the evening and the morning were the third day. Tuesday January 3. Genesis 1:13 (emphasis added)

1

And God said, Let there be lights in the firmament of the heaven to divide the day from the night; and let them be for signs, and for seasons, and for days, and years: And let them be for lights in the firmament of the heaven to give light upon the earth: and it was so. And the evening and the morning were the fourth day. Wednesday January 4.
Genesis 1:13-19 (emphasis added)

There are 4 quarter seasons per year divided into 353 days per year equal 88¼ days per quarter season, please observed these seasons in the beginning months Chart .01 to Chart 1.

And the evening and the morning were the fifth day. Thursday January 5.
Genesis 1:23 (emphasis added)

God created man in his own image, in the image of God created he him; male and female created he them. And the evening and the morning were the sixth day. Adam was created on this day. Friday January 6. Genesis 1:31

And on the seventh day God rested. Saturday January 7.
Genesis 2:2 (emphasis added)

Then, those 7 days became week(s), month(s), and year(s). To reach an undeniable conclusion, we must explain and illustrate those existing facts. A calendar is a document that represent time. It gives validation that a specific event occurred on a certain date, that cannot be refuted when witness by two or more parties. Moses and Aaron both are witnesses of GOWC because they were born within its calendar years. The next recorded time mention by Moses were in years:

And Adam lived an hundred and thirty years, and begat a son in his own likeness, and after his image; and called his name Seth: Genesis 5:3

Moses was writing common knowledge that Adam was created in the first month we call January on Friday 6, GOWC and Seth was born 130 years later on Wednesday January 6, 130 GOWC on Adam created birthday. However, today readers of the scriptures do not have this knowledge of GOWC. Therefore, they must learn this truth. GOWC has 12 months, or 50 weeks and 3 days, or 353 days per year, you can find this in the Strong Exhaustive Concordance for Israel calendar which came from GOWC. Let's learn GOWC from the beginning and let's apply GOWC for Adam lived 11 months the first 3 months has 29 days Charts .01 to .03.

2

GOWC Beginning

Chart .01

1st month January/Tebeth GOWC 3,642 Years 1 Month BC						
Sunday	Monday	Tuesday	Wednesday	Thursday	Friday	Saturday
1 Beginning	2	3	4 Winter	5	6 Adam created	7 God rested
8	9	10	11	12	13	14
15	16	17	18	19	20	21
22	23	24	25	26	27	28
29						

What season was it on the first day, the second day, and the third day in the beginning month Chart .01? None, because the fall season didn't exist yet. This is your first rebuttal that winter do not starts in late December according to your calendar today.

Adam turns 1 month old on Saturday 6, GOWC and Jesus Christ would be born 3,642 GOWC years later Chart .02.

Jesus Christ BC Birth Month

Chart .02

2nd month February/Shebeth 1 month GOWC *3,642 Years BC						
Sunday	Monday	Tuesday	Wednesday	Thursday	Friday	Saturday
*	1	2	3	4	5	6 Adam 1 month old
7	8	9	10	11	12	13
14	15	16	17	18	19	20
21	22	23	24	25	26	27
28	29					

Chart .03

3rd month March/Adar 2 months GOWC 3,642 Years 11 Months BC						
Sunday	Monday	Tuesday	Wednesday	Thursday	Friday	Saturday
		1	2	3	4	5
6 Adam 2 months old	7	8	9	10	11	12
13	14	15	16	17	18	19
20	21	22	23	24	25	26
27	28	29				

The next 9 months alternate from 30 days to 29 days Charts .04 to .12.

Chart .04

4th month April/Abib 3 months GOWC 3,642 Years 10 Months BC						
Sunday	Monday	Tuesday	Wednesday	Thursday	Friday	Saturday
			1	2	3	4
5 Spring	6 Adam 3 months old	7	8	9	10	11
12	13	14	15	16	17	18
19	20	21	22	23	24	25
26	27	28	29	30		

Notice that the beginning spring is **88** days **6** hours from the beginning winter.

Chart .05

5th month May/Zif 4 months GOWC 3,642 Years 9 Months BC						
Sunday	Monday	Tuesday	Wednesday	Thursday	Friday	Saturday
					1	2
3	4	5	6 Adam 4 months old	7	8	9
10	11	12	13	14	15	16
17	18	19	20	21	22	23
24	25	26	27	28	29	

Chart .06

6th month June/Sivan 5 months GOWC 3,642 Years 8 Months BC						
Sunday	Monday	Tuesday	Wednesday	Thursday	Friday	Saturday
						1
2	3	4	5	6 Adam 5 months old	7	8
9	10	11	12	13	14	15
16	17	18	19	20	21	22
23	24	25	26	27	28	29
30						

4

Chart .07

Sunday	Monday	Tuesday	Wednesday	Thursday	Friday	Saturday
7th month July/Tammuz 6 months GOWC 3,642 Years 7 Months BC						
	1	2	3	4	5 Summer	6 Adam 6 months old
7	8	9	10	11	12	13
14	15	16	17	18	19	20
21	22	23	24	25	26	27
28	29					

Notice the beginning summer is 88 days 6 hours from the beginning spring.

Chart .08

Sunday	Monday	Tuesday	Wednesday	Thursday	Friday	Saturday
8th month August/Ab 7 months GOWC 3,642 Years 6 Months BC						
		1	2	3	4	5
6 Adam 7 months old	7	8	9	10	11	12
13	14	15	16	17	18	19
20	21	22	23	24	25	26
27	28	29	30			

Chart .09

Sunday	Monday	Tuesday	Wednesday	Thursday	Friday	Saturday
9th month September/Elul 8 months GOWC 3,642 Years 5 Months BC						
				1	2	3
4	5	6 Adam 8 months old	7	8	9	10
11	12	13	14	15	16	17
18	19	20	21	22	23	24
25	26	27	28	29		

Chart .10

10th month October/Tirshi 9 months GOWC 3,642 Years 4 Months BC						
Sunday	Monday	Tuesday	Wednesday	Thursday	Friday	Saturday
					1	2
3	4	5 Fall	6 Adam 9 months old	7	8	9
10	11	12	13	14	15	16
17	18	19	20	21	22	23
24	25	26	27	28	29	30

Notice that beginning fall is 88 days 6 hours from the beginning summer.

Chart .11

11th month November/ Heshvan 10 months GOWC 3,642 Years 3 Months BC						
Sunday	Monday	Tuesday	Wednesday	Thursday	Friday	Saturday
1	2	3	4	5	6 Adam 10 months old	7
8	9	10	11	12	13	14
15	16	17	18	19	20	21
22	23	24	25	26	27	28
29						

Chart .12

12th month December/Chislef 11 months GOWC 3,642 Years 2 Months BC						
Sunday	Monday	Tuesday	Wednesday	Thursday	Friday	Saturday
	1	2	3	4	5	6 Adam 11 months old
7	8	9	10	11	12	13
14	15	16	17	18	19	20
21	22	23	24	25	26	27
28	29	30				

The days equal 29 days x 7 months equal 203 days plus 30 days x 5 months equal 150 days for a grand total of 353 days per year. Moses and Aaron knew this before the Strong Exhaustive Concordance printed it. As you see today's 365 days calendar do not represent GOWC, therefore today's calendar is totally unprovable mathematically compare to GOWC. Adam turns 1 year old on his twelfth-month in GOWC's first year Chart 1.

Chart 1

1st month January/Tebeth 1 GOWC 3,641 Years 1 Month BC						
Sunday	Monday	Tuesday	Wednesday	Thursday	Friday	Saturday
			1	2	3	4 Winter
5	6 Adam 1 year old	7	8	9	10	11
12	13	14	15	16	17	18
19	20	21	22	23	24	25
26	27	28	29			

Notice that the first-year winter is 88 days 6 hours from the beginning fall. The first three days were going to be the last 3 days in fall, in the first calendar year month January Chart 1. Who but God knew that at creation? Winter to winter was the first seasonal year in GOWC and that has not change, because man cannot change what God created.

Then, notice that the beginning first month Sunday January 1 starts on Wednesday January 1 its first year. This is the third day yearly pattern for the 7 numbers calendar years. So, Wednesday January 1 is the first year, go to Saturday January 1 is the second year, go to Tuesday January 1 is the third year, go to Friday January 1 is the fourth year, go to Monday January 1 is the fifth year, go to Thursday January 1 is the sixth year, go to Sunday January 1 is the seventh year. The third day yearly pattern works for the monthly months and days as well. And every fiscal calendar do the same thing.

Now, let's illustrate that for Adam birthdays including the winter season Charts 2-7.

From Monday last year to Thursday this year Adam turns 2 years old.

Chart 2

1st month January/Tebeth 2 GOWC 3,640 Years 1 Month BC						
Sunday	Monday	Tuesday	Wednesday	Thursday	Friday	Saturday
						1
2	3	4 Winter	5	6 Adam 2 years old	7	8
9	10	11	12	13	14	15
16	17	18	19	20	21	22
23	24	25	26	27	28	29

From Thursday last year to Sunday this year Adam turns 3 years old.

Chart 3

1st month January/Tebeth 3 GOWC 3,639 Years 1 Month BC						
Sunday	Monday	Tuesday	Wednesday	Thursday	Friday	Saturday
		1	2	3	4 Winter	5
6 Adam 3 years old	7	8	9	10	11	12
13	14	15	16	17	18	19
20	21	22	23	24	25	26
27	28	29				

From Sunday last year to Wednesday this year Adam turns 4 years old.

Chart 4

1st month January/Tebeth 4 GOWC 3,638 Years 1 Month BC						
Sunday	Monday	Tuesday	Wednesday	Thursday	Friday	Saturday
					1	2
3	4 Winter	5	6 Adam 4 years old	7	8	9
10	11	12	13	14	15	16
17	18	19	20	21	22	23
24	25	26	27	28	29	

From Wednesday last year to Saturday this year Adam turns 5 years old.

Chart 5

1st month January/Tebeth 5 GOWC 3,637 Years 1 Month BC						
Sunday	Monday	Tuesday	Wednesday	Thursday	Friday	Saturday
	1	2	3	4 Winter	5	6 Adam 5 years old
7	8	9	10	11	12	13
14	15	16	17	18	19	20
21	22	23	24	25	26	27
28	29					

From Saturday last year to Tuesday this year Adam turns 6 years old.

Chart 6

1st month January/Tebeth 6 GOWC 3,636 Years 1 Month BC						
Sunday	Monday	Tuesday	Wednesday	Thursday	Friday	Saturday
				1	2	3
4 Winter	5	6 Adam 6 years old	7	8	9	10
11	12	13	14	15	16	17
18	19	20	21	22	23	24
25	26	27	28	29		

From Tuesday last year to Friday this year Adam turns 7 years old.

Chart 7

1st month January/Tebeth 7 GOWC 3,635 Years 1 Month BC						
Sunday	Monday	Tuesday	Wednesday	Thursday	Friday	Saturday
1	2	3	4 Winter	5	6 Adam 7 years old	7
8	9	10	11	12	13	14
15	16	17	18	19	20	21
22	23	24	25	26	27	28
29						

You can repeat the 7 calendars years to Adam lived 130 years. Or do Adam lived 8 years old on Monday January 6, 8 GOWC; then every seventh year Adam lived 15, 22, 29, 36, 43, 50, 57, 64, 71, 78, 85, 92, 99, 106, 113, 120, 127 years on Monday January 6, GOWC. The next 3 years are;

Adam lived 128 years on Thursday January 6, 128 GOWC.

Adam lived 129 years on Sunday January 6, 129 GOWC.

Adam lived 130 years on Wednesday January 6, 130 GOWC and begot Seth.

Moses wasn't making any random assumption about the first seven days nor Adam lived 130 years and begot Seth. Moses was recording mankind history that have endured unto this day in the scriptures. GOWC was easy to learned and GOWC is perfect!

And ye shall know the truth, and the truth shall make you free.   John 8:32

As you read Jesus was born in zero BC, there are many scriptural principals being used to prove the authenticity of the calendar with the scriptures.

Prove all things; hold fast that which is good.   1 Thessalonians 5:21

For precept must be upon precept, precept upon precept; line upon line, line upon line; here a little, and there a little: Isaiah 28:10

One witness shall not rise up against a man for any iniquity, or for any sin, in any sin that he sinneth: at the mouth of two witnesses, or at the mouth of three witnesses, shall the matter be established.   Deuteronomy 19:15

Every sound doctrine must be proven in the mouth of 2 or 3 witnesses saying the same thing and no doctrine can contradict itself.

Another scripture that is widely used to teach is;

Study to shew thyself approved unto God, a workman that needeth not to be ashamed, rightly dividing the word of truth.   2 Timothy 2:15

Studying the scriptures unto God is more than just reading the scriptures. To rightly divide the word of truth, means the opposite is true too, you can wrongly divide the word of truth. Pro or con you must agree that there are no errors in the beginning. Therefore, if any error(s) found hereafter are correctable that must agree with the beginning.

Then, Moses says;

> And the days of Adam after he had begotten Seth were eight hundred years: and he begat sons and daughters: And all the days that Adam lived were nine hundred and thirty years: and he died. Genesis 5:4, 5

Moses predates Adam lived another 800 years and all days of Adam was 930 years and he died. In Chart 52 the math is given, so Adam died on Tuesday January 6, 930 GOWC on his created birthday. Adam BC date is known that leaves 2,712 Years 24 Days to the birth of Jesus Christ to be exact.

Moses and Aaron both were aware of GOWC on Sunday January/Tebeth 1, 2668 Chart 8 to Chart 8.3.

Chart 8

1st month January/Tebeth 2668 GOWC 974 Years 1 Month BC						
Sunday	Monday	Tuesday	Wednesday	Thursday	Friday	Saturday
			1	2	3	4
5	6	7	8	9	10	11
12	13	14	15	16	17	18
19	20	21	22	23	24	25
26	27	28	29			

Chart 8.1

2nd month February/Shebeth 2668 GOWC *974 Years BC						
Sunday	Monday	Tuesday	Wednesday	Thursday	Friday	Saturday
*				1	2	3
4	5	6	7	8	9	10
11	12	13	14	15	16	17
18	19	20	21	22	23	24
25	26	27	28	29		

Chart 8.2

3rd month March/Adar 2668 GOWC 973 Years 11 Months BC						
Sunday	Monday	Tuesday	Wednesday	Thursday	Friday	Saturday
					1	2
3	4	5	6	7	8	9
10	11	12	13	14	15	16
17	18	19	20	21	22	23
24	25	26	27	28	29	

11

When you read the book of Genesis there was only GOWC, that changed when the Lord said:

> And the Lord spoke unto Moses and Aaron in the land of Egypt saying, This month shall be unto you the beginning of months: it shall be the first month of the year to you.   Exodus 12:1

> And they departed from Rameses in the first month, on the fifteenth day of the first month; on the morrow after the passover the children of Israel went out with an high hand in the sight of all the Egyptians.   Numbers 33:3

God spoke to them on Saturday April/Abib 1, 2668 GOWC and this became After Israel come out of the land of Egypt Calendar (AEC) Chart 8.3.

AEC Beginning

Chart 8.3

1st month April/Abib AEC 4th month April/Abib 2668 GOWC 973 Years 10 Months BC						
Sunday	Monday	Tuesday	Wednesday	Thursday	Friday	Saturday
						1 God speak to Moses and Aaron
2	3	4	5 Spring	6	7	8
9	10 Take lamb	11	12	13	14 The first Passover	15 Left Egypt
16	17	18	19	20	21	22
23	24	25	26	27	28	29
30						

God establish Israel calendar on His day of rest. There are now 2 calendars in the world, separated by 2,668 years 3 months. The AEC has its own BC date which is 973 Years 10 Months. Therefore, Jesus Christ would be born Sunday February/Shebeth 1, 973 AEC. Israel beginning Passover was on Friday April/Abib 14, AEC and Israel left Egypt on Saturday April/Abib 15, AEC Chart 8.3.

Moses continues to give us specific date using the AEC.

> And they took their journey from Elim, and all the congregation of the children of Israel came unto the wilderness of Sin, which is between Elim

12

and Sinai, on the fifteenth day of the second month after their departing out of the land of Egypt. Exodus 16:1

See, for that the Lord hath given you the sabbath, therefore he giveth you on the sixth day the bread of two days; abide ye every man in his place, let no man go out of his place on the seventh day. So the people rested on the seventh day. Exodus 16:29, 30

Chart 9

Sunday	Monday	Tuesday	Wednesday	Thursday	Friday	Saturday
			2nd month May/Zif 1 month AEC 973 Years 9 Months BC			
	1	2	3	4	5	6
7	8	9	10	11	12	13
14	15 Wilderness of Sin	16	17	18	19	20
21	22	23	24	25	26	27 Beginning Sabbath
28	29					

1 Peter 2:2 said, "As new born babes, desire the sincere milk of the word, that you may grow thereby;" once the AEC is established the scriptures clearly identified Israel second month beginning. Then the next scriptures go into years.

And it came to pass in the first month in the second year, on the first day of the month, that the tabernacle was reared up. Exodus 17:1

And the Lord spoke unto Moses in the wilderness of Sinai, in the first month of the second year after they were come out of the land of Egypt, saying, Let the children of Israel also keep the passover at his appointed season. In the fourteenth day of this month, at even, ye shall keep it in his appointed season: Number 9:1-3

Moses gave us 2 dates in the second year first month in those scriptures. Israel beginning month was Saturday April/Abib 1, AEC. The first year was Tuesday April/Abib 1, 1 AEC. The second year was Friday April/Abib 1, 2 AEC and Israel rears up the Tabernacle on Friday the first day and the Passover was on Thursday April/Abib 14, 2 AEC. Those scriptures make you aware that GOWC is still be using, in GOWC this year was April/Abib 2670.

After the death of Moses, God inspired others men to continue writing the scriptures with the AEC dates.

13

And it came to pass in the four hundred and eightieth year after the children of Israel were come out of the land of Egypt, in the month Zif, which is the second month, that he began to build the house of the Lord.
1 Kings 6:1-11:42

Then Solomon began to build the house of the Lord at Jerusalem in mount Moriah, where the Lord appeared unto David his father, in the place that David had prepared in the threshing floor of Ornan the Jebusite. And he began to build in the second day of the second month, in the fourth year of his reign. 1 Chronicles 29:28 to 2 Chronicles 3:2

You need both of those scriptures to understand the total time. Israel is using their AEC in the fourth-year reign of Solomon in the second day of the second month in the four hundred eightieth year after Israel come out of the land of Egypt. Now, let's determine that date mathematically. Israel beginning second month second day is Tuesday May/Zif 2, AEC Chart 9. Therefore, 480 years divided by 7 calendar years equal 68.571. Then, you multiply 68 by 7 equal 476 years on Tuesday May/Zif 2, AEC. The next 4 years are Friday, Monday, Thursday, and finally Sunday May/Zif 2, 480 AEC.

However, before 480 AEC came, there was another fiscal calendar that came into existence call Ab urbe condita (AUC). The Romans empire learned how to create its own AUC fiscal calendar beginning from either GOWC on Sunday March/Adar 1, 2888 years 2 months GOWC or Sunday March/Adar 1, 219 years 11 months AEC. And the AUC calendar is 753 Years 11 Months BC Chart 10.

AUC Calendar Beginning

Chart 10

1st month March/Adar AUC 753 Years 11 Months BC						
Sunday	Monday	Tuesday	Wednesday	Thursday	Friday	Saturday
1	2	3	4	5	6	7
8	9	10	11	12	13	14 Purim
15 Purim	16	17	18	19	20	21
22	23	24	25	26	27	28
29						

Where did the term BC originate from?

A catholic priest named St. Bede in his book entitled Ecclesiastical History of the English People in Chapter 2 he states, "Britain has never been visited by the Romans, and was, indeed, entirely unknown to them before the time of Caius Julius Caesar, who, in the year 693 after the building of Rome, but the sixtieth year before the incarnation of our Lord."

That paragraph tells you that 60 years was on the birth month and date of Jesus Christ in the year 693. You must know these in order to know that 60 Years BC was on Tuesday February/Shebeth 1, 693 AUC Chart 11.

Chart 11

12th month February/Shebeth 693 AUC *60 Years BC						
Sunday	Monday	Tuesday	Wednesday	Thursday	Friday	Saturday
*		1	2	3	4	5
6	7	8	9	10	11	12
13	14	15	16	17	18	19
20	21	22	23	24	25	26
27	28	29				

Jesus Christ was born 60 years later on Sunday February/Shebeth 1, 753 AUC Chart 12.

AD Calendar Beginning

Chart 12

12th month February/Shebeth 753 AUC 1st month February/Shebeth AD						
Sunday	Monday	Tuesday	Wednesday	Thursday	Friday	Saturday
1 Jesus' born	2	3	4	5	6	7
8	9	10	11	12	13	14
15	16	17	18	19	20	21
22	23	24	25	26	27	28
29						

What scholar or non-scholar can deny this truth, that 693 AUC plus 60 Years BC equal 753 AUC is equal to zero BC?

Dionysius Exiguus is credit with devising the Anno Domini (AD) dating system in AD 525. St Bede died May/Zif 26, AD 735. Someone else had to record the death of St. Bede. When you do the math between these 2 years they agree with one another 210 years later with the birthday of Jesus Christ, then you can use that calendar year and determine the day that St. Bede died on Chart 13.

Chart 13

1st month February/Shebeth AD 735						
Sunday	Monday	Tuesday	Wednesday	Thursday	Friday	Saturday
1 Merry Christmas Happy New Year	2	3	4	5	6	7
8	9	10	11	12	13	14
15	16	17	18	19	20	21
22	23	24	25	26	27	28
29						

2nd month March/Adar AD 735						
Sunday	Monday	Tuesday	Wednesday	Thursday	Friday	Saturday
	1	2	3	4	5	6
7	8	9	10	11	12	13
14 Purim	15 Purim	16	17	18	19	20
21	22	23	24	25	26	27
28	29					

3rd month April/Abib AD 735						
Sunday	Monday	Tuesday	Wednesday	Thursday	Friday	Saturday
		1 Rosh Hashana	2	3	4	5 Spring
6	7	8	9	10 Lamb taken	11	12
13	14 Passover	15 Unleavened bread	16	17	18	19
20	21	22	23	24	25	26
27	28	29	30			

4th month May/Zif AD 735						
Sunday	Monday	Tuesday	Wednesday	Thursday	Friday	Saturday
				1	2	3
4	5	6	7	8	9	10
11	12	13	14	15	16	17
18	19	20	21	22	23	24
25	26 St. Bede died	27	28	29		

St. Bede died on these calendars' dates.

5th month Monday May/Zif 26, 4384 GOWC.

2nd month Monday May/Zif 26, 1717 AEC.

3rd month Monday May/Zif 26, 1489 AUC.

Those 4 calendars remain true until around AD 800, that's over 4,400 years of GOWC perfection.

St. Bede book was the first historical book to use the AUC calendar and the BC date for the AD birth of Jesus Christ together.

This book is the second book to used GOWC, the AEC, the AUC calendar, and the BC date for the AD birth of Jesus Christ together; the first book is the Holy Bible!

JESUS WAS BORN

IN ZERO BC

There was in the days of Herod the king of Judaea, a certain priest named Zacharias, of the course of Abia: and his wife was of the daughters of Aaron, and her name was Elisabeth. And it came to pass, that, as soon as the days of his ministration were accomplished, he departed to his own house. And after those days his wife Elisabeth conceived [John the Baptist], *and hid herself five months,*   Luke 1:5, 23-25 emphasis added.

When you read Luke 1:3 he said, "he had perfect understanding of all thing from the very first". Therefore, no dates were unknown to him. He knew the calendar date of Zacharias ministration was from Friday May/Zif 1, 972 AEC to Sunday November/Heshvan 1, 972 AEC. Now, Elisabeth was the cousin to Jesus Christ's mother Mary, she conceived John the Baptist 6 months before Mary and 3 months later she gave birth to John the Baptist, then 6 months later Mary give birth to Jesus Christ. So, we will start at 1 Year 3 Months BC. Elisabeth conceived John the Baptist on Sunday November 1, 752 AUC Chart 14.

18

Chart 14

<table>
<tr><td colspan="7">1 Year 3 Months BC
9th month November 752 AUC
11th month November 3640 GOWC
8th month November 972 AEC</td></tr>
<tr><th>Sunday</th><th>Monday</th><th>Tuesday</th><th>Wednesday</th><th>Thursday</th><th>Friday</th><th>Saturday</th></tr>
<tr><td>1
Elisabeth conceived and hid 5 months</td><td>2</td><td>3</td><td>4</td><td>5</td><td>6</td><td>7</td></tr>
<tr><td>8</td><td>9</td><td>10</td><td>11</td><td>12</td><td>13</td><td>14</td></tr>
<tr><td>15</td><td>16</td><td>17</td><td>18</td><td>19</td><td>20</td><td>21</td></tr>
<tr><td>22</td><td>23</td><td>24</td><td>25</td><td>26</td><td>27</td><td>28</td></tr>
<tr><td>29</td><td></td><td></td><td></td><td></td><td></td><td></td></tr>
</table>

Chart 15

<table>
<tr><td colspan="7">1 Year 2 Months BC
10th month December 752 AUC
12th month December 3640 GOWC
9th month December 972 AEC
Elisabeth hid 1 month*</td></tr>
<tr><th>Sunday</th><th>Monday</th><th>Tuesday</th><th>Wednesday</th><th>Thursday</th><th>Friday</th><th>Saturday</th></tr>
<tr><td></td><td>1*</td><td>2</td><td>3</td><td>4</td><td>5</td><td>6</td></tr>
<tr><td>7</td><td>8</td><td>9</td><td>10</td><td>11</td><td>12</td><td>13</td></tr>
<tr><td>14</td><td>15</td><td>16</td><td>17</td><td>18</td><td>19</td><td>20</td></tr>
<tr><td>21</td><td>22</td><td>23</td><td>24</td><td>25</td><td>26</td><td>27</td></tr>
<tr><td>28</td><td>29</td><td>30</td><td></td><td></td><td></td><td></td></tr>
</table>

Chart 16

<table>
<tr><td colspan="7">1 Year 1 Month BC
11th month January 752 AUC
1st month January 3641 GOWC
10th month January 972 AEC
Elisabeth hid 2 months **</td></tr>
<tr><th>Sunday</th><th>Monday</th><th>Tuesday</th><th>Wednesday</th><th>Thursday</th><th>Friday</th><th>Saturday</th></tr>
<tr><td></td><td></td><td></td><td>1**
Happy New Year</td><td>2</td><td>3</td><td>4
Winter</td></tr>
<tr><td>5</td><td>6</td><td>7</td><td>8</td><td>9</td><td>10</td><td>11</td></tr>
<tr><td>12</td><td>13</td><td>14</td><td>15</td><td>16</td><td>17</td><td>18</td></tr>
<tr><td>19</td><td>20</td><td>21</td><td>22</td><td>23</td><td>24</td><td>25</td></tr>
<tr><td>26</td><td>27</td><td>28</td><td>29</td><td></td><td></td><td></td></tr>
</table>

Chart 17

*1 Year BC 12th month February 752 AUC 2nd month February 3641 GOWC 11th month February 972 AEC Elisabeth hid 3 months***						
Sunday	Monday	Tuesday	Wednesday	Thursday	Friday	Saturday
*				1***	2	3
4	5	6	7	8	9	10
11	12	13	14	15	16	17
18	19	20	21	22	23	24
25	26	27	28	29		

Chart 18

11 Months BC 1st month March 753 AUC 3rd month March 3641 GOWC 12th month March 972 AEC Elisabeth hid 4 months****						
Sunday	Monday	Tuesday	Wednesday	Thursday	Friday	Saturday
					1**** New Year	2
3	4	5	6	7	8	9
10	11	12	13	14 Purim	15 Purim	16
17	18	19	20	21	22	23
24	25	26	27	28	29	

Chart 19

10 Months BC 2nd month April 753 AUC 4th month April 3641 GOWC 1st month April 973 AEC Elisabeth hid 5 months*****						
Sunday	Monday	Tuesday	Wednesday	Thursday	Friday	Saturday
						1***** Rosh Hashana
2	3	4	5 Spring	6	7	8
9	10 Lamb taken	11	12	13	14 Passover	15 Unleavened bread Sabbath
16	17	18	19	20	21	22
23	24	25	26	27	28	29
30						

The calendar month April/Abib above allows you to ask 2 important questions.

1. Did Jesus Christ die on the Good Friday Passover the 14?

2. Did Jesus Christ resurrect early Sunday morning the 16?

The scriptures and the calendars will answer these questions at Jesus Christ death, burial, and resurrection.

After Elisabeth hid for 5 months, the next scriptures said.

> And in the [sixth month] the angel Gabriel was sent from God unto a city of Galilee, named Nazareth, to a virgin espoused to a man whose name was Joseph, of the house of David; and the virgin's name was Mary. And, behold, thy cousin Elisabeth, she hath also conceived a son in her old age: and this is the sixth month with her, who was called barren. And Mary abode with her about three months and returned to her own house.
> Luke 1:26–56

Chart 20

9 Months BC 3rd month May 753 AUC 5th month May 3641 GOWC 2nd month May 973 AEC						
Sunday	Monday	Tuesday	Wednesday	Thursday	Friday	Saturday
	1 Mary Conceived Abode about 3 months	2	3	4	5	6
7	8	9	10	11	12	13
14 Second Passover	15	16	17	18	19	20
21	22	23	24	25	26	27
28	29					

Many pundits believe that in the sixth month was in GOWC months. Others used Israel sixth month, but the scriptures made it clear, that this was Elisabeth sixth month of pregnancy from her conception.

Mary aboded with Elisabeth about 3 months is a specific time from Chart 20 to Chart 22.

Chart 21

			8 Months BC 4th month June 753 AUC 6th month June 3641 GOWC 3rd month June 973 AEC Mary aboded 1 month *			
Sunday	Monday	Tuesday	Wednesday	Thursday	Friday	Saturday
		1*	2	3	4	5
6 Pentecost	7	8	9	10	11	12
13	14	15	16	17	18	19
20	21	22	23	24	25	26
27	28	29	30			

Chart 22

			7 Months BC 5th month July 753 AUC 7th month July 3641 GOWC 4th month July 973 AEC Mary aboded 2 months**			
Sunday	Monday	Tuesday	Wednesday	Thursday	Friday	Saturday
				1**	2	3
4	5 Summer	6	7	8	9	10
11	12	13	14	15	16	17
18	19	20	21	22	23	24
25	26	27	28	29 Mary goes home		

Here is another teaching moment. Jesus said, "Whosoever shall put away his wife, except it be for fornication, and shall marry another, committeth adultery; and whoso marrieth her which is put away doth commit adultery Matthew 19:1. When Mary came home, she was 2 months 28 days pregnant. Here is your exception; Joseph was considering putting Mary away because he thought Mary had committed fornication against him. She was his engaged wife and not his consummated wife, therefore he could have put her away. Fornication is a single person act. And about 3 months means it was 1 day short of 3 months.

Then, the scriptures say,

> Now Elisabeth's full time came that she should be delivered; and she brought forth a son. And her neighbours and her cousins heard how the Lord had shewed great mercy upon her; and they rejoiced with her. *And it came to pass, that on the eighth day they came to circumcise the child*: Luke 1:57-80

Chart 23

			6 Months BC 6th month August 753 AUC 8th month August 3641 GOWC 5th month August 973 AEC			
Sunday	Monday	Tuesday	Wednesday	Thursday	Friday	Saturday
					1 John the Baptist born	2
3	4	5	6	7	8	9 John the Baptist circumcised
10	11	12	13	14	15	16
17	18	19	20	21	22	23
24	25	26	27	28	29	30

In the Introduction there was nothing written about Elisabeth or John the Baptist, so how can any pundit discredit these truths now. Elisabeth had John the Baptist 6 Months BC. John the Baptist was born in the summer season on Friday 1. John the Baptist was circumcised on Saturday 9.

Then,

> Jesus answered and said unto them, "I have done one work, and ye all marvel. Moses therefore gave unto you circumcision; [not because it is of Moses, but of the fathers] and ye on the sabbath day circumcise a man. If a man on the sabbath day receive circumcision, that the law of Moses should not be broken; are ye angry at me, because I have made a man every whit whole on the sabbath day?"   John 7:21–23

Jesus Christ could have been talking about His cousin John the Baptist who was circumcised on the Commandment Sabbath. The Jews could not contradict that truth, since God established that with Abraham when he was 99 years old in 2047 GOWC. Then, the scriptures go silent.

Chart 24

			5 Months BC 7th month September 753 AUC 9th month September 3641 GOWC 6th month September 973 AEC			
Sunday	Monday	Tuesday	Wednesday	Thursday	Friday	Saturday
1	2	3	4	5	6	7
8	9	10	11	12	13	14
15	16	17	18	19	20	21
22	23	24	25	26	27	28
29						

Chart 25

4 Months BC 8th month October 753 AUC 10th month October 3641 GOWC 7th month October 973 AEC						
Sunday	Monday	Tuesday	Wednesday	Thursday	Friday	Saturday
	1	2	3	4	5 Fall	6
7	8	9	10	11	12	13
14	15 Tabernacles	16	17	18	19	20
21	22	23	24	25	26	27
28	29	30				

Chart 26

3 Months BC 9th month November 753 AUC 11th month November 3641 GOWC 8th month November 973 AEC						
Sunday	Monday	Tuesday	Wednesday	Thursday	Friday	Saturday
			1	2	3	4
5	6	7	8	9	10	11
12	13	14	15	16	17	18
19	20	21	22	23	24	25
26	27	28	29			

Chart 27

2 Months BC 10th month December 753 AUC 12th month December 3641 GOWC 9th month December 973 AEC						
Sunday	Monday	Tuesday	Wednesday	Thursday	Friday	Saturday
				1	2	3
4	5	6	7	8	9	10
11	12	13	14	15	16	17
18	19	20	21	22	23	24
25	26	27	28	29	30	

The scripture will clarify when winter is.

> Now the king sat in the winter house in the ninth month: and there was a fire on the hearth burning before him.   Jeremiah 36:22

That scripture shows you that the ninth month is not winter, and the king was only sitting in the winter house on a cold fall day Chart 27.

Chart 28

			1 Month BC 11th month January 753 AUC 1st month January 3642 GOWC 10th month January 973 AEC			
Sunday	Monday	Tuesday	Wednesday	Thursday	Friday	Saturday
						1 Happy New Year
2	3	4 Winter	5	6	7	8
9	10	11	12	13	14	15
16	17	18	19	20	21	22
23	24	25	26	27	28	29

The scriptures take us to the birth of Jesus Christ.

Joseph also went up from Galilee, To be taxed with Mary his espoused wife, being great with child. And so it was, that, while they were there, the days were accomplished that she should be delivered. And she brought forth her firstborn son, and wrapped him in swaddling clothes, and laid him in a manger; And there were in the same country shepherds abiding in the field, keeping watch over their flock by night. And the angel said unto them, Fear not: for, behold, I bring you good tidings of great joy, which shall be to all people. For unto you is born this day in the city of David a Saviour, which is Christ the Lord. And when eight days were accomplished for the circumcising of the child, his name was called Jesus, which was so named of the angel before he was conceived in the womb.   Luke 2:1 – 2:40

Merry Christmas and Happy New Year

Chart 29

			1st month February AD 12th month February 753 AUC 11th month February 973 AEC 2nd month February 3642 GOWC			
Sunday	Monday	Tuesday	Wednesday	Thursday	Friday	Saturday
1 Jesus born	2	3	4	5	6	7
8	9 Jesus circumcised	10	11	12	13	14
15	16	17	18	19	20	21
22	23	24	25	26	27	28
29						

25

At the birth of Jesus Christ became Merry Christmas and Happy New Year because at His birth fulfilled them both. Jesus Christ was circumcised on Monday February/Shebeth 9, AD.

We now have 4 calendars dates for the birth of Jesus Christ. This is very important because;

> At the mouth of two witnesses, or three witnesses, shall he that is worthy of death be put to death; but at the mouth of one witness he shall not be put to death. Deuteronomy 17:6

> But if he will not hear thee, then take with thee one or two more, that in the mouth of two or three witnesses every word may be established. Matthew 18:16

> This is the third time I am coming to you. In the mouth of two or three witnesses shall every word be established. 2 Corinthians 13:1

In the mouth of 2 or 3 witnesses is a doctrine that established the truth because 1 witness even when true cannot established the truth. These ancient historians Titus Flavius Josephus, Dionysius Exiguus, and St. Bede knew when Jesus Christ was born. The 4 calendars are witnesses to the truth, especially St. Bede calendar date which is historically known. Jesus was born in zero BC verified the truth from the errors in this information you can find in the Wikipedia on-line encyclopedia.

The year AD 1 corresponds to AUC 754, based on the epoch of Varro. Thus:

AUC	Year	Event
1	753 BC	Foundation of the Kingdom of Rome
244	510 BC	Overthrow of the Roman monarchy
259	495 BC	Death in exile of King Lucius Tarquinius Superbus
490	264 BC	Punic Wars
709	45 BC	First year of the Julian calendar
710	44 BC	The assassination of Julius Caesar
727	27 BC	Augustus became the first Roman emperor
753	1 BC	Astronomical Year 0
754	AD 1	Approximate birth date of Jesus, approximated by Dionysius Exiguus in AD 525 (AUC 1278)

Many pundits love to debate the birth of Jesus Christ with their prowess, but their prowess will go in vain. When you analyze that information, they had reliable sources of time from Varro, Exiguus, and St. Bede, but they misinterpreted those reliable sources. Whoever tried to convert the BC years into the AUC calendar years didn't know the birth month of Jesus Christ, nor the AUC calendar month beginning. Look at 1 AUC is 753 BC and 753 AUC is 1 BC, their events dates are wrong as stated; 752 AUC is 1 BC and 753 AUC is their Astronomical Year 0 for the birth of Jesus Christ AD. And when you move the miss place approximate birth date of Dionysius Exiguus of Jesus Christ above to St. Bede proper date of 753 AUC and add Dionysius Exiguus AD 525 equal (1278 AUC) from the birth of Jesus Christ. That's why Jesus was born in zero BC presents those truths for your perusing and because the scriptures with the calendars speaks louder than any pundit prowess Chart 29.

THE

AGES OF

JESUS CHRIST!

The foundation has been laid, there is nothing, that can be added, that will not agree with the birth of Jesus Christ. According to the epoch of Varro AD 1 is 754 AUC this is true, because 12 months later from Jesus Christ birth He was 1 year old. This historical data was never lacking, only those who wrote after them couldn't interpret their calendar dates.

Then, the scriptures say,

> Now when Jesus was born in Bethlehem of Judaea in the days of Herod the king, behold, there came wise men from the east to Jerusalem, Saying, where is he that is born King of the Jews? Then Herod, when he had privily called the wise men, enquired of them diligently what time the star appeared. And when they were come into the house, the saw the young child with Mary his mother, and fell down, and worshipped him: and when they had opened their

treasures, they presented unto him gifts; gold, and frankincense and myrrh. Then Herod, when he saw that he was mocked of the wise men, was exceeding wroth, and sent forth, and slew all the children that were in Bethlehem, and in all the coasts thereof, from two years old and under, according to the time which he had diligently inquired of the wise men. Matthew 2:18

These wise men did not appear at Jesus nativity scene, that is widely believe by most, but they came to a house, to a young child. These wise men said, "Where is he that is born King of the Jew" why is this an important statement? Because every king from king Saul to Jesus Christ was born on February 1. This is the reason why the birthday of Jesus Christ was important; it was a qualification that all the prior kings had and all of Israel knew that. These wise men were probably using GOWC and king Herod had to convert that calendar into his calendar and he determine Jesus Christ was 2 years old Chart 30.

Jesus Christ 2 Years Old

Chart 30

1st month February AD 2 12th month February 755 AUC 2nd month February 3644 GOWC 11th month February 975 AEC						
Sunday	Monday	Tuesday	Wednesday	Thursday	Friday	Saturday
						1 Merry Christmas Happy New Year
2	3	4	5	6	7	8
9	10	11	12	13	14	15
16	17	18	19	20	21	22
23	24	25	26	27	28	29

Now his parents went to Jerusalem every year at the feast of the Passover. And when he was twelve years old, they went up to Jerusalem after the custom of the feast. And when they had fulfilled the days, as they returned, the child Jesus tarried behind in Jerusalem; and Joseph and his mother knew not of it. *But they, supposing him to have been in the company, went a day's journey;* and they sought him among their kinsfolk and acquaintance. *And when they found him not, they turned back again to Jerusalem, seeking him. And it came to pass, that after three days they found him in the temple,* sitting in the midst of the doctors, both hearing them, and asking them questions. And Jesus increased in wisdom and stature, and in favour with God and man. Luke 2:41–52 emphasis added

Jesus Christ was a child of 12 years old before the New Year Passover that occurred 2 months 13 days later. Now, you can use those scriptures in the calendar month below and determine whether you agree or not. You can see, if your interpretation agrees with this: The feast of Unleavened bread started on Wednesday April 15; it ended on Wednesday April 22. His parents left on Thursday April 23 and they took a day journey out that's Friday April 24. It took them a day journey to get back to Jerusalem that's Saturday April 25. After 3 days is the fourth day. They found Jesus in the Temple of God on Wednesday April 29 Chart 31.

Jesus Christ was 12 Years Old

Chart 31

3rd month April AD 12 2nd month April 766 AUC 4th month April 3664 GOWC 1st month April 986 AEC						
Sunday	Monday	Tuesday	Wednesday	Thursday	Friday	Saturday
			1 Rosh Hashana	2	3	4
5 Spring	6	7	8	9	10 Lamb taken	11
12	13	14 Passover	15 Unleavened bread	16	17	18
19	20	21	22 Unleavened bread end	23 Parents leaves	24 1 day out	25 1 day back
26 After 1 day	27 After 2 days	28 After 3 days	29 Jesus in the Temple	30		

Depending on the reader knowledge, you may or may not understand the synoptic account of Matthew, Mark, and Luke and sometime John. Since, John did not mention many of the same events that Matthew, Mark, and Luke did together, scholars thought John was sometime, but they are one.

Now in the fifteenth year of the reign of Tiberius Caesar, Pontius Pilate being governor of Judaea, and Herod being tetrarch of Galilee, and his brother Philip tetrarch of Ituraea and of the region of Trachonitis, and Lysanias the tetrarch of Abilene, Annas and Caiaphas being the high priests, the word of God came unto John the son of Zacharias in the wilderness. And he came into all the country about Jordan, preaching the baptism of repentance for the remission of sins; *As it is written in the book of the words of Esaias the prophet, saying, The voice of one crying in the wilderness, Prepare ye the way of the Lord, make his paths straight.*   Luke 3:1-4

The voice of one crying in the wilderness, Prepare ye the way of the Lord, make his paths straight.   Mark 1:1-5

The voice of one crying in the wilderness, Prepare ye the way of the Lord, make his paths straight. Matthew 3:1-6

He said, I am the voice of one crying in the wilderness, Make straight the way of the Lord, as said the prophet Esaias. John 1:5-23

All 4 Gospel are represented in Tiberius Caesar reigned, stated as AD 14 to AD 37, he was in his fifteenth year reigned making John the Baptist ministry to commence in AD 29 on his thirtieth birthday Chart 32.

John the Baptist Ministry Begins

Chart 32

7th month August AD 29 8th month August 3671 GOWC 5th month August 1003 AEC 6th month August 783 AUC						
Sunday	Monday	Tuesday	Wednesday	Thursday	Friday	Saturday
				1 John the Baptist 30 yrs. old	2	3
4	5	6	7	8	9	10
11	12	13	14	15	16	17
18	19	20	21	22	23	24
25	26	27	28	29	30	

Temple of God Completed

Chart 33

8th month September AD 29 7th month September 783 AUC 6th month September 1003 AEC 9th month September 3671 GOWC *John the Baptist 1 month baptizing						
Sunday	Monday	Tuesday	Wednesday	Thursday	Friday	Saturday
						1*
2	3	4	5	6	7	8
9	10	11	12	13	14	15
16	17	18	19	20	21	22
23	24 Temple of God completed	25	26	27	28	29

31

But when the fulness of the time was come, God sent forth his Son, made of a woman, made under the law, To redeem them that were under the law, that we might receive the adoption of sons.   Galatians 4:4, 5

Then cometh Jesus from Galilee to Jordan unto John, to be baptized of him. Then was Jesus led up of the Spirit into the wilderness to be tempted of the devil. Matthew 3:13-4:1

And it came to pass in those days, that Jesus came from Nazareth of Galilee, and was baptized of John in Jordan. And immediately the spirit driveth him into the wilderness.   Mark 1:9-12

Now when all the people were baptized, it came to pass, that Jesus also being baptized, and praying, the heaven was opened, And the Holy Ghost descended in a bodily shape like a dove upon him, and a voice came from heaven, which said, Thou art my beloved Son; in thee I am well pleased. *And Jesus himself began to be about thirty years of age*, being [as was supposed] the son of Joseph, which was the son of Heli [God]. And Jesus being full of the Holy Ghost returned from Jordan, and was led by the Spirit into the wilderness.   Luke 3:21-4:1

John the Baptist baptized the people for 5 months 28 days. God truly confirmed His word when He used the word −about− 30 years old as done with Mary when she aboded −about− 3 months with Elisabeth and the next day was 3 months. Jesus Christ was baptized 1 day before His 30 birthday Chart 34.

Jesus Christ about 30 Years Old

Chart 34

12th month January AD 29 11th month January 783 AUC 10th month January 1003 AEC 1st month January 3672 GOWC *John the Baptist 5 months baptizing						
Sunday	Monday	Tuesday	Wednesday	Thursday	Friday	Saturday
					1* Happy New Year	2
	4 Winter	5	6	7	8	9
10	11	12	13	14	15	16
17	18	19	20	21	22	23
24	25	26	27	28	29 Jesus baptized	

Being forty days tempted of the devil. And in those days, he did eat nothing. Luke 4:2-12

And he was there in the wilderness forty days, tempted of Satan. Mark 1:13

And when he had fasted forty days and forty nights, he was afterward an hundred.   Matthew 4:2

Jesus Christ 30 Years Old

Chart 35

Sunday	Monday	Tuesday	Wednesday	Thursday	Friday	Saturday
1st month February AD 30						

1st month February AD 30 12th month February 783 AUC 2nd month February 3672 GOWC 11th month February 1003 AEC						
Sunday	Monday	Tuesday	Wednesday	Thursday	Friday	Saturday
						1 Merry Christmas and Happy New Year
2	3	4	5	6	7	8
9	10	11	12	13	14	15
16	17	18	19	20	21	22
23	24	25	26	27	28	29

The next scriptures are after Jesus thirtieth birthday.

And when the devil had ended all the temptation, he departed from him for a season. And Jesus returned in the power of the Spirit into Galilee. Luke 4:13, 14

The devil departed from Jesus for a season. How long is a season?

Thou shalt therefore keep this ordinance in his season from year to year. Exodus 13:10

So, the next time Jesus speak to the devil that will be 1 year on the same month and date Matthew 16:23.

The 40 days and 40 nights solidified the birthday of Jesus Christ from His baptismal. On Saturday February 29 this was 29 days of the 40 days and 40 nights, March 11 is the fortieth day. Jesus Christ returns from the wilderness on Wednesday March/Adar 11 Chart 36.

33

God account for the rest of that month as follows:

Thursday March 12

The next day John seeth Jesus coming unto him, and saith, Behold the Lamb of God, which taketh away the sin of the world. Again, the next day after John stood, and two of his disciples; And looking upon Jesus as he walked, he saith, Behold the Lamb of God!   John 1:29-36

John the Baptist sees Jesus twice on March 12 Chart 36.

Friday March 13

The day following Jesus would go forth into Galilee, and findeth Philip, and saith unto him, Follow me.   John 1:43

Saturday March 14

And the third day there was a marriage in Cana of Galilee, and the mother of Jesus was there.   John 2:1

John account for the first 3 days after Jesus' return from the wilderness. Then the scriptures continue to build on these trues.

Sunday March 15 to Saturday March 21

And he came to Nazareth, where he had been brought up: and, as his custom was, he went into the synagogue on the sabbath day, and stood up for to read. Luke 4:16

Sunday March 22 to Sunday March 29

And came down to Capernaum, a city of Galilee, and taught them on the sabbath days.   Luke 4:31

Sunday March 22 to Sunday March 29

After this he went down to Capernaum, he, and his mother, and his brethren, and his disciples: and they continued there not many days.   John 2:12

Chart 36

Chart 36

		2nd month March AD 30 1st month March 784 AUC 3rd month March 3672 GOWC 12th month March 1003 AEC				
Sunday	Monday	Tuesday	Wednesday	Thursday	Friday	Saturday
1 Happy New Year	2	3	4	5	6	7
8	9	10	11 40 days ended the devil departed	12 Jesus sees John twice today	13 Jesus finds Philip	14 Marriage Purim
15 Purim Jesus read scriptures	16	17	18	19	20	21
22	23	24	25	26	27	28
29						

If, you look at Sunday March 15 you will notice it was considered a Sabbath day. Mordecai and Esther established a 2 days' rest on March 14 and 15 in (Esther 9:20-29) it is called Purim now you can do a check and balance with the first Purim mention with no scriptures referenced in 973 AEC Chart 18 and the math is true 31 years later Chart 36.

> And the Jews' Passover was at hand, and Jesus went up to Jerusalem. Jesus answered and said unto them, Destroy this temple, and in three days I will raise it up. Then said the Jews, Forty and six years was this temple in building, and wilt thou rear it up in three days? But he spoke of the temple of his body. When therefore he was risen from the dead, his disciples remembered that he had said this unto them; and they believed the scripture, and the word which Jesus had said. Now when he was in Jerusalem at the Passover, in the feast day, many believed in his name, when they saw the miracles which he did.   John 2:13–23 emphasis added

The Jews told Him the Temple of God took 46 years to complete, as if, Jesus did not know that?

When you focus on the Gospel of John, he takes you through the require feast days that every male must attend in a year.

> Three times thou shalt keep a feast unto me in the year. Thou shalt keep the feast of unleavened bread: (thou shalt eat unleavened bread seven, as I commanded thee, in the time appointed of the month Abib; for in it thou camest out from Egypt: and none shall appear before me empty:) And the feast of harvest, the first fruits of thy labours, which thou hast sown in the

field: and the feast of ingathering, which is in the end of the year, when thou hast gathered in thy labours out of the field. Three times in the year all thy males shall appear before the Lord God.   Exodus 23:14-17

The 3 feasts are the feast of Unleavened bread on April 15, the feast of Pentecost on June 6, and the feast of Tabernacles on October 15. The Gospel of John is working through the 3 feast days. Now you can understand that John was the boundary that Matthew, Mark, and Luke were contain in by feast days. The feast of Unleavened bread is done, 2 more feast days to do in this year.

Chart 37

	3rd month April AD 30 4th month April 3672 GOWC 1st month April 1004 AEC 2nd month April 784 AUC					
Sunday	Monday	Tuesday	Wednesday	Thursday	Friday	Saturday
	1 Rosh Hashana	2	3	4	5 Spring	6
7	8	9	10 Lamb taken	11	12	13
14 Passover	15 Unleavened bread	16	17	18	19	20
21	22	23	24	25	26	27
28	29	30				

When the scriptures said Jesus was about 30 years old, means you should know when He was 30 years old and you can prove it? Jesus was 2 years old on Saturday than 28 years later He was 30 years old on Saturday. When Jesus Christ was 12 years old at the Passover on Tuesday 14 mean 18 years later Jesus Christ was 30 years old at the Passover on Sunday 14. Let's prose a question.

Did Jesus' attend 3 more yearly Passover in His earthly ministry? If, He did than He would be 33 years old at the Passover of His death and burial. This is an important question that Jesus was born in zero BC answer unequivocally. The scriptures harmonized themselves, when you rightly divide the word of truth.

And it came to pass on the second Sabbath after the first, that he went through the corn fields; and his disciples plucked the ears of corn, and did eat, rubbing them in their hands. And certain of the Pharisees said unto them, Why do ye that which is not lawful to do on the Sabbath days? Luke 6:1–2

36

At that time Jesus went on *the Sabbath day through the corn*; and his disciples were an hungred, and began *to pluck the ears of corn* and to eat. But when the Pharisees saw it, they said unto him, Behold, thy disciples do that which is not lawful to do upon the Sabbath day.
Matthew 12:1, 2 (italics added)

And it came to pass, that he went through the *cornfields on the Sabbath day*; and his disciples began, as they went, to pluck the ears of corn. And the Pharisees said unto him, Behold, why do they on the Sabbath day that which is not lawful…And he said unto them, The Sabbath was made for man, and not man for the Sabbath.   Mark 2:23, 24, 27

When we look at Luke, Matthew, and Mark, the second Sabbath after the first Sabbath tell us they are all on the same day Chart 38.

Israel had a second Passover on May/Zif 14, for those who could not keep the first Passover. You can read it for yourself in Number 9:1-13. Jesus gives us the feast of Tabernacles.

Say not ye, There are yet four months, and then cometh harvest? Behold, I say unto you, Lift up your eyes, and look on the fields; for they are white already to harvest.   John 4:35 (italics added)

Many pundits symbolized the literal meaning of the scriptures wrongly. Jesus was giving the disciples the third feast day that every male must attend in a year the feast of Tabernacles on October 15, John 7:2. So, Jesus spoke John 4:35 on May 15, Chart 38.

Second Sabbath After the First

Chart 38

4th month May AD 30 3rd month May 784 AUC 5th month May 3672 GOWC 2nd month May 1004 AEC 5 months to Tabernacles *****						
Sunday	Monday	Tuesday	Wednesday	Thursday	Friday	Saturday
			1	2	3	4 First Sabbath
5	6	7	8	9	10	11 Second Sabbath
12	13	14 Second Passover	15 ***** Jesus predates the feast of Tabernacles	16	17	18
19	20	21	22	23	24	25
26	27	28	29			

After this there was a feast of the Jews; and Jesus went up to Jerusalem.
John 5:1

What feast day was this? Many scholars teach this feast day as another year Passover. However, this feast day is Pentecost the second feast day that every male must attend in a year on June 6, Chart 39. When your ideology is wrong, then you force the scriptures to say what they are not saying because of your desire to be right.

The scriptures keep you from making calendar year errors.

Chart 39

Sunday	Monday	Tuesday	Wednesday	Thursday	Friday	Saturday
5th month June AD 30 4th month June 784 AUC 6th month June 3672 GOWC 3rd month June 1004 AEC 4 months to Tabernacles ****						
				1	2	3
4	5	6 Pentecost	7	8	9	10
11	12	13	14	15 ****	16	17
18	19	20	21	22	23	24
25	26	27	28	29	30	

Chart 40

Sunday	Monday	Tuesday	Wednesday	Thursday	Friday	Saturday
6th month July AD 30 7th month July 3672 GOWC 4th month July 1004 AEC 5th month July 784 AUC 3 months to Tabernacles ***						
						1
2	3	4	5 Summer	6	7	8
9	10	11	12	13	14	15***
16	17	18	19	20	21	22
23	24	25	26	27	28	29

At that time Herod the tetrarch heard of the fame of Jesus, And said unto his servants, This is John the Baptist; he is risen from the dead; and therefore mighty works do shew forth themselves in him. But when Herod's birthday was kept, the daughter of Herodias danced before them, and pleased Herod. Whereupon he promised with an oath to give her whatsoever she would ask. And she, being before instructed of her mother, said, Give me here John Baptist's head in a charger. And the king was sorry: nevertheless for the oath's sake, and them which sat with him at meat, he commanded it to be given her. And he sent, and beheaded John in the prison. And his head was brought in a charger, and given to the damsel: and she brought it to her mother. And his disciples came, and took up the body, and buried it, and went and told Jesus.   Matthew 14:1–12

And king Herod heard of him; [for his name was spread abroad] and he said, That John the Baptist was risen from the dead, and therefore mighty works do shew forth themselves in him. Others said, That it is Elias. And others said, That it is a prophet, or as one of the prophets. But when Herod heard thereof, he said, It is John, whom I beheaded: he is risen from the dead. For Herod himself had sent forth and laid hold upon John, and bound him in prison for Herodias' sake, And when a convenient day was come, that Herod on his birthday made a supper to his lords, high captains, and chief estates of Gaillee.   Mark 6:14–21

Now Herod the tetrarch heard of all that was done by him: and he was perplexed, because that it was said of some, that John was risen from the dead; And of some, that Elias had appeared; and of others, that one of the old prophets was risen again. And Herod said, John have I beheaded: but who is this, of whom I hear such things? And he desired to see him. Luke 9:7–9

And they that had eaten were about five thousand men, beside women and children.   Matthew 14:21

And they that did eat of the loaves were about five *thousand men.* Mark 6:44 emphasis added

For they were about *five thousand* men and he said to his disciples. Make them sit down by fifties in a company.   Luke 9:14 emphasis added

And Jesus said, Make the men sit down. Now there was much grass in the place. So the men sat down, in number about *five thousand.*   John 6:10

He was a burning and a shining light: and ye were willing for a season to rejoice in his light.   John 5:35

You must read the scriptures with the knowledge of words meaning, that simplified your interpretation. A season is year to year, therefore Jesus told you John the Baptist ministry was 1 year from AD 29 to AD 30 and John the Baptist was 31 years old when he was beheaded Chart 41.

Notice, that Matthew, Mark, Luke, and John all mention Jesus feeding the 5 thousand. Why is this important, this show you that their witness is orderly and not jumping backward and forward. This is the common mistake when you read the Gospel of Jesus Christ separately instead of collectively.

John the Baptist Killed

Chart 41

John the Baptist born Friday August 1, 6 Months BC John the Baptist killed Sunday August 1, AD 30 John the Baptist born Friday August 1, 753 AUC John the Baptist killed Sunday August 1, 784 AUC John the Baptist born Friday August 1, 3641 GOWC John the Baptist killed Sunday August 1, 3672 GOWC John the Baptist born Friday August 1, 973 AEC John the Baptist killed Sunday August 1, 1004 AEC 2 months to Tabernacles **						
Sunday	Monday	Tuesday	Wednesday	Thursday	Friday	Saturday
1 John the Baptist killed	2	3	4	5	6	7 Tisha B" AV Feed five thousand
8	9	10	11	12	13	14
15 **	16	17	18	19	20	21
22	23	24	25	26	27	28
29	30					

After the death of John the Baptist, Jesus Christ is now 6 months away from His 31 birthday.

Chart 42

8th month September AD 30 7th month September 784 AUC 9th month September 3672 GOWC 6th month September 1004 AEC 1 month to Tabernacles *						
Sunday	Monday	Tuesday	Wednesday	Thursday	Friday	Saturday
		1	2	3	4	5
6	7	8	9	10	11	12
13	14	15 *	16	17	18	19
20	21	22	23	24 Temple Anniversary	25	26
27	28	29				

The Temple of God turns 1 year old Thursday September 24, 1004 AEC.

And in the seventh month, on the first day of the month, ye shall have an holy convocation; ye shall do no servile work: it is a day of blowing the trumpets unto you. Numbers 29:1

Also on the tenth day of this seventh month there shall be a day of atonement: it shall be an holy convocation unto you; and ye shall afflict your souls, and offer an offering made by fire unto the Lord. Leviticus 23:27

Speak unto the children of Israel, saying, The fifteenth day of this seventh month shall be the feast of tabernacles for seven days unto the Lord. Leviticus 23:34

Now the Jew's feast of tabernacles was at hand. On the last and greatest day of the Feast, Jesus stood and said in a loud voice, If anyone is thirsty, let him come to me and drink. John 7:2-7

God did not change the Jewish holidays dates that do not agree with scriptures. When you gain knowledge of scriptures dates, they must agree with the calendar present, past, and future like these prior feast days these are natural check and balances for any calendar year.

John 7:2-7 the feast of Tabernacles proves those prior feast days were in this same year.

Tabernacles

Chart 43

9th month October AD 30 8th month October 784 AUC 10th month October 3672 GOWC 7th month October 1004 AEC						
Sunday	Monday	Tuesday	Wednesday	Thursday	Friday	Saturday
			1 Blowing of Trumpets	2	3	4
5 Fall	6	7	8	9	10 Yom Kippur	11
12	13	14	15 Tabernacles	16	17	18
19	20	21	22 Last day Jesus speak	23	24	25
26	27	28	29	30		

41

Chart 44

				10th month November AD 30		
				9th month November 784 AUC		
				11th month November 3672 GOWC		
				8th month November 1004 AEC		
Sunday	Monday	Tuesday	Wednesday	Thursday	Friday	Saturday
					1	2
3	4	5	6	7	8	9
10	11	12	13	14	15	16
17	18	19	20	21	22	23
24	25	26	27	28	29	

Chart 45

				11th month December AD 30		
				10th month December 784 AUC		
				12th month December 3672 GOWC		
				9th month December 1005 AEC		
Sunday	Monday	Tuesday	Wednesday	Thursday	Friday	Saturday
						1
2	3	4	5	6	7	8
9	10	11	12	13	14	15
16	17	18	19	20	21	22
23	24	25	26	27	28	29
30						

And it was at Jerusalem the feast of the dedication, and it was winter. John 10:22

We know God created the beginning season winter on Wednesday January/Tebeth 4, GOWC. John identified the feast of Dedication with winter because both were on the same date.

Chart 46

				12th month January AD 30		
				11th month January 784 AUC		
				1st month January 3673 GOWC		
				10th month January 1004 AEC		
Sunday	Monday	Tuesday	Wednesday	Thursday	Friday	Saturday
	1 Happy New Year	2	3	4 Winter Dedication Hanukkah	5	6
7	8	9	10	11	12	13
14	15	16	17	18	19	20
21	22	23	24	25	26	27
28	29					

Jesus Christ 31 Years Old

Chart 47

1st month February AD 31 12th month February 784 AUC 2nd month February 3673 GOWC 11th month February 1004 AEC						
Sunday	Monday	Tuesday	Wednesday	Thursday	Friday	Saturday
		1 Merry Christmas Happy New Year	2	3	4	5
6	7	8	9	10	11	12
13	14	15	16	17	18	19
20	21	22	23	24	25	26
27	28	29				

You cannot deny Jesus Christ 30 years old birthday from His baptismal. Now, Jesus Christ is 31 years old.

> Get thee behind me, Satan: thou art an offence unto me; for thou savourest not the things that be of God, but those that be of men. Matthew 16:23

This is a paramount statement that have been missed, after the devil departed from Jesus for a season, this is 1 year later on Saturday March 11, 1005 AEC. After Jesus return from the wilderness, you can't find another scripture where Jesus speaks to the devil in Matthew, Mark, Luke or John before that scripture.

The next 2 scriptures are given for time agreement in that month.

> And after six days Jesus taketh Peter, James, and John his brother, and bringeth them up into an high mountain apart, And was transfigured before them: and his face did shine as the sun, and his raiment was white as the light.   Matthew 17:1, 2

> And after six days Jesus taketh with him Peter, and James, and John, and leadeth them up into an high mountain apart by themselves: and he was transfigured before them.   Mark 9:2

Then the scriptures said after 6 days, this simply mean the seventh day when Jesus Christ was transfigured Chart 48.

Lazarus Sick and Died

Now a certain man was sick, named Lazarus, of Bethany, the town of Mary and her sister Martha. (It was that Mary which anointed the Lord with ointment, and wiped his feet with her hair, whose brother Lazarus was sick.) Therefore his sisters sent unto him, saying, Lord, behold, he whom thou lovest is sick. John 11:1-6

Chart 48

2nd month March AD 31 3rd month March 3673 GOWC 12th month March 1004 AEC 1st month March 785 AUC						
Sunday	Monday	Tuesday	Wednesday	Thursday	Friday	Saturday
			1 Happy New Year	2	3	4
5	6	7	8	9	10	11 Jesus speak to the devil
12	13	14 Purim	15 Purim	16	17	18 Jesus transfigured
19	20	21	22	23	24	25
26	27	28 Lazarus died	29			

When Jesus heard that, he said, This sickness is not unto death, but for the glory of God, that the Son of God might be glorified thereby. Now Jesus loved Martha, and her sister, and Lazarus. When he had heard therefore that he was sick, he abode two days still in the same place where he was. John 11:1-6

Thursday April 1

Jesus' abode 1 day.

Friday April 2

Jesus' abode 2 days.

Saturday April 3

Then when Jesus came, he found that he had lain in the grave four days already [Lazarus died on Tuesday March 28]... And one of them, named Caiaphas, being the high priest that same year, said unto them, Ye know nothing at all, Nor consider that it is expedient for us, that one man should

die for the people, and that the whole nation perish not. And this spake he not of himself: but being high priest that year, he prophesied that Jesus should die for that nation; And not for that nation only, but that also he should gather together in one the children of God that were scattered abroad.
John 11:7-52

These scriptures tell you this was a New Year. Jesus rosed Lazarus from the dead on the first Commandment Sabbath in a New Year.

Jesus was born in zero BC was learned from why Jesus didn't resurrect on Easter Sunday from this.

This young Muslim came to me one day and spoke.

"Clarence, the Bible isn't true."

"Why" I asked him.

"Do you believe Jesus Christ died on Good Friday and rose early Sunday morning?"

"Yes," I replied.

He immediately responded, "Jesus said in Matthew 12:40 'Like Jonas was in the belly of the great fish three days and three nights so shall the Son of Man be three days and three nights in the heart of the earth.' And Friday to early Sunday morning isn't three days and three nights." He smiled, then nonchalantly walked away from me.

I was dumbfounded, how do you get three days and three nights from Friday to early Sunday morning? You can't and I never, even, thought about it, until this young Muslim mention it.

Here why, because the pastor said, "Jesus was buried on Friday, He was in the grave all-day Saturday, but early Sunday morning He got up with all power in heaven and in earth."

You hear 3 days, but it wasn't 3 complete days. So, I went straight to God, and said, "God, he's right. Friday to early Sunday morning is not 3 days and 3 nights, and if there is one lie in the Bible then it's all a lie." Jesus also mention He would rise the third day. So, where are the 3 days and the 3 nights? It's in the scriptures when you rightly divide the word of truth.

One day while reading the Bible and I read this;

> Then Jesus six days before the Passover came to Bethany, where Lazarus was which had been dead, whom he raised from the dead.   John 12:1-11

From reading this scripture you can count the days to the Passover through the scriptures when you rightly divide the word of truth.

> On the next day much people that were come to the feast, when they heard that Jesus was coming to Jerusalem.   John 12:12

On the next day, the Gospel of John was 5 days before the Passover. Then John skip days and goes to 2 days before the Passover John 12:37. When you read the Gospel separately, you believe each Gospel is giving their own unique perspective, instead of a collaboration of witnesses as one Gospel. The Gospel of Jesus Christ was a puzzle that had to be put together by Matthew, Mark, Luke, and John Gospel to count the 6 days before the Passover and the 3 days and 3 nights to Jesus Christ resurrection.

However, many Christians who read their Bible, do not know the date of the Passover and the feast of Unleavened bread sabbath.

> And in the fourteenth day of the first month is the passover of the Lord. And in the fifteenth day of this month is the feast: seven days shall Unleavened Bread be eaten. In the first day shall be an holy convocation; ye shall do no manner of servile work therein: Numbers 28:16-18

The Jewish Passover is on April/Abib 14, AEC and the Unleavened bread sabbath follow the Passover every year on April/Abib 15, AEC. Here is where you learn how to put the days to the dates for Jesus Christ death, burial, and resurrection.

Six days before the Passover is:

April 8

When you read that scripture, you do not know the day, just the date. And on the next day you still do not know the day, just the date is the 9 and John, Matthew, Mark, and Luke mention Palm Day on April 9.

April 9

On the next day much people that were come to the feast, when they heard that Jesus was coming to Jerusalem. Took branches of palm trees, and went forth to meet him, and cried, Hosanna: Blessed is the King of Israel that cometh in the name of the Lord.   John 12:12-36

April 9

And brought the ass, and the colt, and put on them their clothes, and they set him thereon. And a very great multitude spread their garments in the way; others cut down branches from the trees, and strowed them in the way. And the multitudes that went before, and that followed, cried, saying, Hosanna to the son of David: Blessed is he that cometh in the name of the Lord; Hosanna in the highest. And he left them, and went out of the city into Bethany; and he lodged there.   Matthew 21:1-17

April 9

And they brought him to Jesus: and they cast their garments upon the colt, and they set Jesus thereon. And as he went, they spread their clothes in the way. And when he was come nigh, even now at the descent of the mount of Olives, the whole multitude of the disciples began to rejoice and praise God with a loud voice for all the mighty works that they had seen; Saying, Blessed be the King that cometh in the name of the Lord: peace in heaven, and glory in the highest. Luke 19:29-46

April 9

And they brought the colt to Jesus, and cast their garments on him; and he sat upon him. And many spread their garments in the way: and others cut down branches off the trees, and strowed them in the way. And they that went before, and they that followed, cried, saying, Hosanna; Blessed is he that cometh in the name of the Lord: Blessed be the kingdom of our father David, that cometh in the name of the Lord: Hosanna in the highest. And. Jesus entered into Jerusalem, and into the temple: and when he had looked round about upon all things, and now the eventide was come, he went out unto Bethany with the twelve.   Mark 11:1-11

The beginning and the ending of the nineth day is clearly stated, Jesus leaves Jerusalem and spend the night in Bethany with the twelve.

April 10

Now the next day, when they were come from Bethany, he was hungry. And when even was come, he went out of the city.   Mark 11:12 – 19

April 10

Now in the morning as he returned into the city, he hungered.
Matthew 21:18 – 19

April 10

And in the day time he was teaching in the temple; and at night he went out, and abode in the mount that is called the mount of Olives.
Luke 20:1 – 21:37

Mark says, "Now the next day," just like John did. There can be no confusion that we are now 4 days before the Passover. Again, the scriptures plainly tell us Jesus Christ daily routine.

April 11

And in the morning as they passed by, they saw the fig tree dried up from the roots.   Mark 11:20 – 13:37

April 11

And when the disciples saw it, they marveled, saying, How soon is the fig tree withered away. Ye know that after two days is the feast of the Passover, and the Son of man is betrayed to be crucified.   Matthew 21:20 – 26:2

We are now 3 days before the Passover. On April 11 Jesus plainly tell us exactly what will happen to Him on the third day, the Passover on April 14 when He would be betrayed to be crucified.

April 12

After two days was the feast of the Passover, and of unleavened bread (on the 15). But they said, Not on the feast day, lest there be an uproar of the people.   Mark 14:1-2 emphasis added

Mark used the same terminology after 2 completed days is the third day. April 15 was the Passover and the feast of Unleavened bread.

April 12

And all the people came early in the morning to him in the temple, for to hear him.   Luke 21:38

April 12

Not on the feast day, lest there be an uproar among the people.
Matthew 26:3-5

April 12

But though he had done so many miracles before them, yet they believed not on him: That the saying of Esaias the prophet might be fulfilled, which he spake, Lord, who hath believed our report? and to whom hath the arm of the Lord been revealed?   John 12:37-50

The Gospel of John was observing until April 12. We are 2 days before the Passover. When you read the Gospel of John by itself, you probably would have read right through John 12:37-50 April 12 verses to John 13:1 because April 12 was hard to see by itself, if you were not studying, to rightly divide the word of truth.

April 13

Now before the feast of the Passover, when Jesus knew that his hour was come that he should depart out of this world unto the Father, having loved his own which were in the world, he loved them unto the end.   John 13:1

One day before the Passover John, Matthew, Mark, and Luke mention this day.

April 13

Now when Jesus was in Bethany, in the house of Simon the leper, There came unto him a woman having an alabaster box of very precious ointment, and poured it on his head, as he sat at meat.   Matthew 26:6-16

April 13

And being in Bethany in the house of Simon the leper, as he sat at meat, there came a woman having an alabaster box of ointment of spikenard very precious; and she brake the box, and poured it on his head.   Mark 14:3-11

April 13

Now the feast of unleavened bread drew nigh, which is called the Passover. Luke 22:1-6

The scriptures always plainly state what they mean.

In the fourteenth day of the first month at even is the Lord's passover. And on the fifteenth day of the same month is the feast of Unleavened bread to the Lord; seven days you must eat unleavened bread. On the first day you shall have a holy convocation; you shall do no customary work on it. Leviticus 23:5-7

April 14 the Passover

Now the first day of the feast of unleavened bread the disciples came to Jesus, saying unto him, Where wilt thou that we prepare for thee to eat the Passover? Then Pilate commanded the body to be delivered. And when

Joseph had taken the body… And laid it in his own new tomb…and he rolled a great stone to the door of the sepulcher, and departed.
Matthew 26:17-27:61

April 14 the Passover

And the first day of unleavened bread, when they killed the Passover, his disciples said unto him, Where wilt thou that we go and prepare that thou mayest eat the Passover? And now when the even was come, because it was the preparation, that is, the day before the sabbath,... And Pilate… gave the body to Joseph…and laid him in a sepulcher which was hewn out of a rock, and rolled a stone unto the door of the sepulcher.   Mark 14:12−15:47

April 14 the Passover

Then came the day of unleavened bread, when the Passover must be killed. And he sent Peter and John, saying, Go and prepare us the Passover, that we may eat. And they said unto him, Where wilt thou that we prepare? This man went unto Pilate, and begged the body of Jesus. And he took it down, and wrapped it in linen, and laid it in a sepulcher that was hewn in stone, wherein never man before was laid. And that day was the preparation, and the sabbath drew on.   Luke 22:7-23:55

April 14 the Passover

And supper being ended, the devil having now put into the heart of Judas Iscariot, Simon's son, to betray him; Jesus knowing that the Father had given all things into his hands, and that he was come from God, and went to God. The Jews therefore, because it was the preparation, that the bodies should not remain upon the cross on the sabbath day, (for that sabbath day was an high day,) besought Pilate that their legs might be broken, and that they might be taken away. Then took they the body of Jesus, and wound it in linen clothes with the spices, as the manner of the Jews is to bury. Now in the place where he was crucified there was a garden; and in the garden a new sepulcher…There laid they Jesus.   John 13:2-19:42

That was 6 days before the Passover.

The apostle Paul says,

Moreover, brethren, I declare unto you the gospel which I preached unto you, which also ye have received, and wherein ye stand; By which also ye are saved if ye keeping memory what I preached unto you, unless ye have believed in vain. For I delivered unto you first of all that which I also received, how that Christ died for our sins according to the Scriptures; And that he was buried, and the he rose again the third day according to the Scriptures.   1 Corinthians 15:1–4

The apostle Paul said, Jesus Christ death, burial, and resurrection was according to the scriptures. Now, let's do the 3 days and 3 nights.

April 15, the first day in the grave, Unleavened bread Sabbath

Now the next day, that followed the day of the preparation, the chief priests and Pharisees came together unto Pilate. Saying, Sir, we remember that that deceiver said, while he was yet alive, After three days I will rise again. Command therefore that the sepulcher be made sure until the third day (17), lest his disciples come by night (17), and steal him away,
Matthew 27:62-66 emphasis added

April 16, the second day in the grave

Now when the Sabbath was past, Mary Magdalene, Mary the mother of James, and Salome bought spices, that they might come and anoint Him. Mark 16:1

Then they returned and prepared the spices and fragrant oils. And they rested on the Sabbath according to the commandment.   Luke 23:56

April 17, the third day in the grave, Commandment Sabbath

That was 3 days and 3 nights in the grave for Jesus Christ. Jesus Christ resurrected on the Commandment Sabbath, just like He rose Lazarus from the dead on the Commandment Sabbath. Matthew, Mark, Luke, and John honor the Commandment Sabbath by not writing anything on that day. Matthew, Mark, Luke, and John showed you that they are synchronized because all the witnesses go back to writing on the first day of the week.

Sunday April 18

Now after the Sabbath, as the first day of the week began to dawn, Mary Magdalene and the other Mary came to see the tomb. And when they were assembled with the elders, and had taken counsel, they gave large money unto the soldiers, Saying, Say ye, His disciples came by night (17), and stole him away while we slept.   Matthew 28:1-15 emphasis added

Sunday April 18

Now on the first day of the week, very early in the morning, they, and certain other women with them, came to the tomb bringing the spices which they had prepared. But we trusted that it had been he which should have redeemed Israel: and beside all this, **today is the third day since these things were done**.   Luke 24:1-21

51

Sunday April 18

Very early in the morning, on the first day of the week, they came to the tomb when the sun had risen.   Mark 16:2-9

Sunday April 18

Now on the first day of the week Mary Magdalene went to the tomb early, while it was still dark, and saw that the stone had been taken away from the tomb. And after eight days. … John 20:1-26

Tuesday April 27

… again his disciples were within, and Thomas with them: then came Jesus, the doors being shut, and stood in the midst, and said, Peace be unto you. Then saith he to Thomas, Reach hither thy finger, and behold my hands; and reach hither thy hand, and thrust it into my side: and be not faithless, but believing. And Thomas answered and said unto him, My Lord and my God. John 20:26…31

The apostle Paul said, according to the scriptures, what apostle, what prophet, what evangelist, what pastor, what teacher have proven any of this according to the calendars. Remember the calendar day was from evening to evening, as you look at these events below.

Jesus Christ 6 Days Before Passover

Chart 49

1st month April 1005 AEC Jesus killed Wednesday April 14, AD 31 Jesus resurrected Saturday April 17, AD 31						
Sunday	Monday	Tuesday	Wednesday	Thursday	Friday	Saturday
				1 Rosh Hashana Jesus' aboded 1 day	2 Jesus aboded 2 days	3 Jesus raised Lazarus from the dead
4	5 Spring	6	7	8 6 days before Passover	9 Palm Friday	10 Lamb taken Fig tree cursed
11 See cursed fig tree After 2 days is Passover	12 After 2 days was Passover and Unleavened bread	13 Before Passover	14 Is Passover Jesus crucified and bury around 5 pm	15 Was Passover and Unleavened bread Sabbath Set guards at Jesus In tomb 1 day and 1 night in heart of	16 Women bought prepared spices and fragrant oils Jesus 2 days and 2 nights in heart of the earth 5 pm	17 Women rested Commandment Sabbath Jesus 3 days and 3 nights in heart other earth Jesus Christ resurrection 5 pm

				the earth 5 pm		
18 First day is today 3rd day	19	20	21	22	23	24
25	26	27 Thomas sees Jesus	28	29	30	

At the age of 31 years 2 months 13 days old Jesus Christ was our Passover lamb of the first year slain from the foundation of the world!

Jesus Christ Ascends into Heaven

The former treatise have I made, O Theophilus, of all that Jesus began both to do and teach, Until the day in which he was taken up, after that he through the Holy Ghost had given commandments unto the apostles whom he had chosen: To whom also he shewed himself alive after his passion by many infallible proofs, being seen of them forty days, and speaking of the things pertaining to the kingdom of God: And, being assembled together with them, commanded them that they should not depart from Jerusalem, but wait for the promise of the Father, which, saith he, ye have heard of me. For John truly baptized with water; **but ye shall be baptized with Holy Ghost not many days hence.** And while they looked steadfastly toward heaven as he went up, behold, two men stood by them in white apparel; Which also said, Ye men of Galilee, why stand ye gazing up into heaven? this same Jesus, which is taken up from you into heaven, shall so come in like manner as ye have seen him go into heaven. Then returned they unto Jerusalem from the mount called Olivet, which is from Jerusalem a sabbath day's journey. Acts 1:1-12

Jesus Christ was seen for 40 days before He ascended into heaven. What day was that? 5 weeks of Sunday times 7 days equal 35 days plus 5 days equal Friday May 28, Chart 50.

Chart 50

4th month May AD 31 5th month May 3673 GOWC 2nd month May 1005 AEC 3rd month May 785 AUC						
Sunday	Monday	Tuesday	Wednesday	Thursday	Friday	Saturday
						1
2	3	4	5	6	7	8
9	10	11	12	13	14 Second Passover	15
16	17	18	19	20	21	22
23	24	25	26	27	28 Jesus ascends into heaven	29 Sabbath

And when the day of Pentecost was fully come, they were all with one accord in one place.   Acts 2:1

Chart 51

5th month June AD 31 6th month June 3673 GOWC 3rd month June 1005 AEC 4th month 785 AUC						
Sunday	Monday	Tuesday	Wednesday	Thursday	Friday	Saturday
1 Sabbath journey end	2	3	4	5	6 Pentecost Filled with Holy Ghost	7
8	9	10	11	12	13	14
15	16	17	18	19	20	21
22	23	24	25	26	27	28
29	30					

The apostles arrived in Jerusalem on Sunday June 1, that ended their Sabbath day journey.

Pentecost is the second feast day that every male must attend, this prove that John 5:1 was Pentecost without being name specifically last year Chart 39.

In the ministry of Jesus Christ there are no ambiguities in the scriptures. But men hold the truth in unrighteousness because they love their ungodly deeds. Wherefore, when you continue to adhere to the truth you get more truth. For example, the scriptures teach time. From the scriptures above "not many days" is 7 days from Jesus' ascension to Pentecost. Therefore, when you see that same wording in John 2:12 and Luke 15:13 those are 7 days too.

When you study the Gospel of Jesus Christ, very little is even written of all the things He did. The calendar magnifies that truth and this scripture states it clearly.

And there are also many other things which Jesus did, the which, if they should be written every one, I suppose that even the world itself could not contain the books that should be written. Amen.   John 21:25

All the books in the world today, is like a grain of a mustard seed in comparison to what John has stated. Jesus Christ did so much more in the 1 year 2 months and 13 days of His earthly ministry is incomprehensible.

THE

CALENDARS

The purpose of this chapter is to prove the calendar years from the beginning to Jesus was born in zero BC that's 3,642 years 1 month GOWC.

> In the beginning God created the heaven and the earth. And God said, Let us make man in our image, after our likeness: And the evening and the morning were the sixth day. And Adam lived an hundred and thirty years, and begat a son in his own likeness, and after his image; and called his name Seth: And the days of Adam after he had begotten Seth were eight hundred years: and he begat sons and daughters: And all the days that Adam lived were nine hundred and thirty years: and he died.   Genesis 1:1...31, 5:1-5

Adam lived these years on Monday January 6; 1, 8, 15, 22, 29, 36, 43, 50, 57, 64, 71, 78, 85, 92, 99, 106, 113, 120, 127 years. The next 3 GOWC years were Thursday 6, 128 GOWC; Sunday January 6, 129 GOWC; and Wednesday January 6, 130 GOWC and Seth was born. God predates Adam lived another 800 years to Tuesday January 6, 930 GOWC and Adam died; the remaining BC date is 2,712 Years and 24 Days from Adam death to the birth of Jesus Christ.

Chart 52 contains the 130 years Adam lived follow by the 800 years Adam lived in that sequential order. This Chart allow the reader to count the accuracy for those 930 years.

GOWC Beginning

Chart 52

Adam created January 6, GOWC 3,642 Years 24 Days BC						
Sunday	Monday	Tuesday	Wednesday	Thursday	Friday	Saturday
1 Beginning	2	3	4 Winter	5	6 Adam created	7 God rested
Adam lived 130 January 6, GOWC 3,512 Years 24 Days BC						
			1	2	3	4 Winter
5	6 Adam lived	7	8	9	10	11
1, 8, 15, 22, 29, 36, 43, 50, 57, 64, 71, 78, 85, 92, 99, 106, 113, 120, 127,						

Sunday	Monday	Tuesday	Wednesday	Thursday	Friday	Saturday
	6 Adam lived 127			6 Adam lived 128		
6 Adam lived 129			6 Adam lived 130 Seth born			

Adam lived 800 Years January 6, GOWC 2,712 Years 24 Days BC						
Sunday	Monday	Tuesday	Wednesday	Thursday	Friday	Saturday
			6 Adam lived 130			6 Adam lived 1,
8, 15, 22, 29, 36, 43, 50, 57, 64, 71, 78, 85, 92, 99, 106, 113, 120, 127, 134, 141, 148, 155, 162, 169, 176, 183, 190, 197, 204, 211, 218, 225, 232, 239, 246, 253, 260, 267, 274, 281, 288, 295, 302, 309, 316, 323, 330, 337, 344, 351, 358, 365, 372, 379, 386, 393, 400, 407, 414, 421, 428, 435, 442, 449, 456, 463, 470, 477, 484, 491, 498, 505, 512, 519, 526, 533, 540, 547, 554, 561, 568, 575, 582, 589, 596, 603, 610, 617, 624, 631, 638, 645, 652, 659, 666, 673, 680, 687, 694, 701, 708, 715, 722, 729, 736, 743, 750, 757, 764, 771, 778, 785, 792, 799,						

January 930 GOWC						
Sunday	Monday	Tuesday	Wednesday	Thursday	Friday	Saturday
				1	2	3
4 Winter	5	6 Adam lived 800	7	8	9	10
11	12	13	14	15	16	17
18	19	20	21	22	23	24
25	26	27	28	29		

It's all math, as long as you count through the years in the scriptures correctly your end result will be the same because we know $a^2+b^2=c^2$, that mathematical equation that do not lie. Notice that 930 GOWC year started on Thursday and Adam died as stated 800 years later on Tuesday January 6, and all the days of Adam was 930 years. Now, you can leisurely prove Jesus Christ was born Sunday February 1 through the scriptures.

> And Seth lived an hundred and five years, and begat Enos: And Seth lived after he begat Enos eight hundred and seven years, and begat sons and daughters: And all the days of Seth were nine hundred and twelve years: and he died.   Genesis 5:6-8

Seth 130 birth year was added to Seth 105 years lived equal Seth lived these years on Saturday January 6; 1, 8, 15, 22, 29, 36, 43, 50, 57, 64, 71, 78, 85, 92, 99 years. The next 6 years were Tuesday January 6, 230 GOWC; Friday January 6, 231 GOWC; Monday January 6, 232 GOWC; Thursday January 6, 233 GOWC; Sunday January 6, 234 GOWC; and Wednesday January 6, 235 GOWC and Enos was born. God predates Seth lived another 807 years to Tuesday January 6, 1042 GOWC and Seth died; the BC year is 2,600.

> And Enos lived ninety years, and begat Cainan: And Enos lived after he begat Cainan eight hundred and fifteen years, and begat sons and daughters: And all the days of Enos were nine hundred and five years: and he died. Genesis 5:9–11

Enos 235 birth year was added to Enos 90 years lived equal Enos lived these years on Saturday January 6; 1, 8, 15, 22, 29, 36, 43, 50, 57, 64, 71, 78, 85 GOWC years and the next 5 years were Tuesday January 6, 321 GOWC, Friday January 6, 322 GOWC, Monday January 6, 323 GOWC, Thursday January 6, 324 GOWC, and Sunday January 6, 325 GOWC and Cainan was born. Then, God predates the death of Enos as done with Adam and Seth.

Enos lived 815 years on Tuesday January 6, 1140 GOWC and he died; the BC year is 2,502.

> And Cainan lived seventy years and begat Mahalaleel: And Cainan lived after he begat Mahalaleel eight hundred and forty years, and begat sons and daughters. And all the days of Cainan were nine hundred and ten years: and he died.   Genesis 5:12-14

Cainan 325 birth years was added to Cainan 70 years lived equal Mahalaleel born Sunday January 6, 395 GOWC. Cainan died Sunday January 6, 1235 GOWC and 2407 BC.

> And Mahalaleel lived sixty and five years, and begat Jared. And Mahalaleel lived after he begat Jared eight hundred and thirty years, and begat sons and daughters: And all the days of Mahalaleel were eight hundred ninety and five years: and he died.   Genesis 5:15-17

Mahalaleel 395 birth years was added to Mahalaleel 65 years lived equal Jared born Saturday January 6, 460 GOWC. Mahalaleel died Thursday January 6, 1290 GOWC and 2352 BC.

> And Jared lived an hundred sixty and two years, and he begat Enoch: And Jared lived after he begat Enoch eight hundred years, and begat sons and daughters: And all the days of Jared were nine hundred sixty and two years: and he died.   Genesis 5:18-20

Jared 460 birth years was added to Jared 162 years lived equal Enoch born Tuesday January 6, 622 GOWC. Jared died Monday January 6, 1422 GOWC and 2220 BC.

> And Enoch lived sixty and five years, and begat Methuselah: And Enoch walked with God after he begat Methuselah three hundred years, and begat sons and daughters: And all the days of Enoch were three hundred sixty and five years: And Enoch walked with God: and he was not; for God took him. Genesis 5:21–24

Enoch 622 birth years was added to Enoch 65 years lived equal Methuselah born Monday January 6, 687 GOWC. Enoch walked with God on Friday January 6, 987 GOWC and 2655 BC.

> And Methuselah lived an hundred eighty and seven years, and begat Lamech. And Methuselah lived after he begat Lamech seven hundred eighty and two years, and begat sons and daughters: And all the days of Methuselah were nine hundred sixty and nine years: and he died.   Genesis 5:25–27

Methuselah 687 birth years was added to Methuselah 187 years lived equal Lamech born Tuesday January 6, 874 GOWC. Methuselah died in the year of the Flood on Wednesday January 6, 1656 GOWC and 1986 BC.

Adam died 56 years after the birth of Lamech on Tuesday January 6, 930 GOWC this prove that all of the predated death years after Adam must be true according to the calendar.

> And Lamech lived an hundred eighty and two years, and begat a son: And he called his name Noah, saying, Tis same shall comfort us concerning our work and toil of our hands, because of the ground which the Lord hath cursed. And Lamech lived after he begat Noah five hundred ninety and five years, and begat sons and daughters: And all the days of Lamech were seven hundred seventy and seven years: and he died.   Genesis 5:28–31

Lamech 874 birth years was added to Lamech 182 years lived equal Noah born Tuesday January 6, 1056 GOWC Chart 53.

> And Noah was five hundred years old: and Noah begat Shem, Ham, and Japheth.   Genesis 5:32

The Life of Noah

Chart 53

Noah born Tuesday January 6, 1056 GOWC						
Sunday	Monday	Tuesday	Wednesday	Thursday	Friday	Saturday
		Noah born			Noah lived	
50, 57, 64, 71, 78, 85, 92, 99, 106, 113, 120, 127, 134, 141, 148, 155, 162, 169, 176, 183, 190, 197, 204, 211, 218, 225, 232, 239, 246, 253, 260, 267, 274, 281, 288, 295, 302, 309, 316, 323, 330, 337, 344, 351, 358, 365, 372, 379, 386, 393, 400, 407, 414, 421, 428, 435, 442, 449, 456, 463, 470, 477, 484, 491, 498,					1, 8, 15, 22, 29, 36, 43,	
Sunday	Monday	Tuesday	Wednesday	Thursday	Friday	Saturday
	Noah 499 years old			Noah 500 Japheth born 1056		
Ham born 1057			Shem born 1058			

> And the Lord said unto Noah, Come thou and all thy house into the ark; for thee have I seen righteous before me in this generation. *For yet seven days, and I will cause it to rain upon the earth forty days and forty nights*; and every living substance that I have made will I destroy from off the face of the earth. And Noah did according unto all that the Lord commanded him. ***And Noah was six hundred years old when the flood of waters was upon the earth.***   Genesis 7:1, 4-6 emphasis added

Chart 54

			Noah 500 Thursday January 6, 1556 GOWC			
			Noah lived 600 Wednesday January 6, 1656 GOWC			
Sunday	Monday	Tuesday	Wednesday	Thursday	Friday	Saturday
				6th Noah 500		
Noah lived						
1, 8, 15, 22, 29, 36, 43, 50, 57, 64, 71, 78, 85, 92, 99,						
Sunday	Monday	Tuesday	Wednesday	Thursday	Friday	Saturday
			Noah 600 years old			

God through Moses take us from the first day to 1656 GOWC, the 600 birthdays of Noah, without showing us GOWC. Methuselah death was predated on Noah birthday too Chart 55.

Chart 55

			1st month January 1656 GOWC			
			1986 Years 1 Month BC			
Sunday	Monday	Tuesday	Wednesday	Thursday	Friday	Saturday
					1 Happy New Year	2
3	4 Winter	5	6 Noah 600 years old	7	8	9
10	11	12	13	14	15	16
17	18	19	20	21	22	23
24	25	26	27	28	29	

*And it came to pass after seven days, that the waters of the flood were upon the earth. In the six hundredth year of Noah in the second month, the seventeenth day of the month, the same day were all the fountains of the great deep broken up, and the windows of heaven were opened. And the rain was upon the earth forty days and forty nights. In the selfsame day entered Noah, and Shem, and Ham, and Japheth, the sons of Noah, and Noah's wife, and the three wives of his sons with them, into the ark; And they that went in, went in male and f emale of all flesh, as God had commanded him: and the Lord shut him in. And the flood was forty days upon the earth; and the waters increased, and bare up the ark, and it was lift up above the earth. And every living substance was destroyed which was upon the face of the ground, both man, and cattle, and the creeping things, and the fowl of the heaven; and they were destroyed from the earth: and Noah only remained alive, and they that were with him in the ark And the waters prevailed upon the earth an hundred and fifty days.
Genesis 9:21- 26*

Now, let's the scriptures prove that the calendar year is 353 days per year. From Friday January 1, 1656 GOWC to the Flood Monday February 17, 1656 GOWC is 45 days plus from the Flood is another 150 days that the water prevailed on the earth equal 195 days.

Chart 56

2nd month February 1656 GOWC *1986 BC						
Sunday	Monday	Tuesday	Wednesday	Thursday	Friday	Saturday
*						1
2	3	4	5	6	7	8
9 After 7 days	10	11	12	13	14	15
16	17 The Flood	18	19	20	21	22
23	24	25	26	27	28	29

Chart 57

3rd month March 1656 GOWC 1986 Years 11 Months BC						
Sunday	Monday	Tuesday	Wednesday	Thursday	Friday	Saturday
1	2	3	4	5	6	7
8	9	10	11	12	13	14
15	16	17	18	19	20	21
22	23	24	25	26	27	28 Rain 40 days
29						

Chart 58

4th month April 1656 GOWC 1986 Years 10 Months BC						
Sunday	Monday	Tuesday	Wednesday	Thursday	Friday	Saturday
	1	2	3	4	5 Spring	6
7	8	9	10	11	12	13
14	15	16	17	18	19	20
21	22	23	24	25	26	27
28	29	30				

Chart 59

5th month May 1656 GOWC 1986 Years 9 Months BC						
Sunday	Monday	Tuesday	Wednesday	Thursday	Friday	Saturday
			1	2	3	4
5	6	7	8	9	10	11
12	13	14	15	16	17	18
19	20	21	22	23	24	25
26	27	28	29			

Chart 60

6th month June 1656 GOWC 1986 Years 8 Months BC						
Sunday	Monday	Tuesday	Wednesday	Thursday	Friday	Saturday
				1	2	3
4	5	6	7	8	9	10
11	12	13	14	15	16	17
18	19	20	21	22	23	24
25	26	27	28	29	30	

The fountains also of the deep and the windows of heaven were stopped, and the rain from heaven was restrained; and the waters returned from off the earth continually: **and after the end of the hundred and fifty days the waters were abated. And the ark rested in the seventh month, on the seventeenth day of the month, upon the mountains of Ararat. And the waters decreased continually until the tenth month:** Genesis 7:25—8:4

Chart 61

7th month July 1656 GOWC 1986 Years 7 Months BC						
Sunday	Monday	Tuesday	Wednesday	Thursday	Friday	Saturday
						1
2	3	4	5 Summer	6	7	8
9	10	11	12	13	14	15
16	17 Ark rested	18	19	20 Water prevailed 150 days	21	22
23	24	25	26	27	28	29

Chart 62

8th month August 1656 GOWC 1986 Years 6 Months BC						
Sunday	Monday	Tuesday	Wednesday	Thursday	Friday	Saturday
1	2	3	4	5	6	7
8	9	10	11	12	13	14
15	16	17	18	19	20	21
22	23	24	25	26	27	28
29	30					

Chart 63

9th month September 1656 GOWC 1986 Years 5 Months BC						
Sunday	Monday	Tuesday	Wednesday	Thursday	Friday	Saturday
		1	2	3	4	5
6	7	8	9	10	11	12
13	14	15	16	17	18	19
20	21	22	23	24	25	26
27	28	29				

In the tenth month, on the first day of the month, were the tops of the mountains seen.   Genesis 8:5

Chart 64

10th month October 1656 GOWC 1986 Years 4 Months BC						
Sunday	Monday	Tuesday	Wednesday	Thursday	Friday	Saturday
			1 Mountains seen	2	3	4
5 Fall	6	7	8	9	10	11
12	13	14	15	16	17	18
19	20	21	22	23	24	25
26	27	28	29	30		

And it came to pass at the end of forty days, that Noah opened the window of the ark which he had made: And he sent forth a raven, which went forth to and from, until the waters were dried up from off the earth. Also he sent forth a dove from him, to see if the waters were abated from off the face of the ground; But the dove found no rest for the sole of her foot, and she returned unto him into the ark, for the waters were on the face of the whole earth: then he put forth his hand, and took her, and pulled her in unto him into the ark. And he stayed yet other seven days; and again he sent forth the dove out of the ark; And the dove came into him in the evening; and, lo, in her mouth was an olive leaf pluck off: so Noah knew that the waters were abated from off the earth. And he stayed yet other seven days; and sent forth the dove; which returned not again unto him anymore.   Genesis 8:6—12

Chart 65

11th month November 1656 GOWC 1986 Years 3 Months BC						
Sunday	Monday	Tuesday	Wednesday	Thursday	Friday	Saturday
					1	2
3	4	5	6	7	8	9
10	11 Noah open window	12	13	14	15	16
17	18 Yet seven days	19	20	21	22	23
24	25 Yet seven days	26	27	28	29	

Chart 66

			12th month December 1656 GOWC 1986 Years 2 Months BC			
Sunday	Monday	Tuesday	Wednesday	Thursday	Friday	Saturday
						1
2	3	4	5	6	7	8
9	10	11	12	13	14	15
16	17	18	19	20	21	22
23 Water abated 150 days	24	25	26	27	28	29
30						

We have 195 days plus another 150 days for the water abatement equal 345 days and that's 8 days short of a New Year, and the number 8 stand for a New Beginning.

> And it came to pass in the six hundredth and first year, in the first month, the first day of the month, the waters were dried up *from off* the earth: and Noah removed the covering of the ark, and looked, and, behold, the face of the ground was dry.   Genesis 8:13 emphasis added

Chart 67

			1st month January 1657 GOWC 1985 Years 1 Month BC			
Sunday	Monday	Tuesday	Wednesday	Thursday	Friday	Saturday
	1 Happy New Year Ground dried	2	3	4 Winter	5	6
7	8	9	10	11	12	13
14	15	16	17	18	19	20
21	22	23	24	25	26	27
28	29					

That scripture clearly states, that this year was before Noah 601 birthday. So, now we have the first month and the first day of the month Monday January 1, 1657 GOWC. That's 245 days plus 8 days equal 353 days per year from the scriptures.

> **And in the second month, on the seven and twentieth day of the month, was the earth dried.** And God spoke unto Noah, saying, Go forth of the ark, thou, and thy wife, and thy sons, and thy sons' wives with thee. Genesis 8:14-16

64

Chart 68

2nd month February 1657 GOWC *1985 BC						
Sunday	Monday	Tuesday	Wednesday	Thursday	Friday	Saturday
*		1	2	3	4	5
6	7	8	9	10	11	12
13	14	15	16	17	18	19
20	21	22	23	24	25	26
27 Earth dried	28	29				

Moses mention both the Flood date on Monday February 17, 1656 GOWC and the earth was dried on Sunday February 27, 1657 GOWC this is over a new fiscal calendar year. So, from Monday February 17, 1656 GOWC to Thursday February 17, 1657 GOWC must equal 12 months and 353 days.

And the reversal is true too. Sunday February 27, 1657 GOWC is mention and last year it wasn't, but that date must be Thursday February 27, 1656 GOWC Chart 56. That makes GOWC provable and cannot be denied, especially when you consider this was over 1,657 years later from the beginning first day. Now can you deny GOWC birth for Jesus Christ 2063 years later from Chart 56?

And Noah lived after the flood three hundred and fifty years. And all the days of Noah were nine hundred and fifty years: and he died.
Genesis 9:28, 29 emphasis added

Chart 69

After the Flood began on Thursday February 17, 1657 GOWC Noah died Monday February 17, 2006 GOWC						
Sunday	Monday	Tuesday	Wednesday	Thursday	Friday	Saturday
		1	2	3	4	5
6	7	8	9	10	11	12
13	14	15	16	17 After Flood	18	19

1, 8, 15, 22, 29, 36, 43, 50, 57, 64, 71, 78, 85, 92, 99, 106, 113, 120, 127, 134, 141, 148, 155, 162, 169, 176, 183, 190, 197, 204, 211, 218, 225, 232, 239, 246, 253, 260, 267, 274, 281, 288, 295, 302, 309, 316, 323, 330, 337, 344,

Sunday	Monday	Tuesday	Wednesday	Thursday	Friday	Saturday
345			346			347
		348			349	
	Noah lived 350 died 950					

The scriptures made no mention of Noah 601 birthday in the year 601 GOWC and in the first month. That is why, you must pay attention to the wording in the scriptures. It said Noah lived after the Flood 350 years. If Noah would have celebrated his 601 birthdays on Saturday January 6, 1657 GOWC, Noah would have been 951 years old at his death on Monday February 17, 2006 GOWC.

These are the generations of Shem: Shem was a hundred years old, and begat Arphaxad two years after the flood.   Genesis 10:22

Chart 70

Sunday	Monday	Tuesday	Wednesday	Thursday	Friday	Saturday
Shem born Wednesday January 6, 1558 GOWC Shem lived Tuesday January 6, 1658 GOWC 1984 Years 24 days BC						
			6 Shem born			6 Shem lived
99, 92, 85, 78, 71, 64, 57, 50, 43, 36, 29, 22, 15, 8, 1						
January 1658 GOWC						
Sunday	Monday	Tuesday	Wednesday	Thursday	Friday	Saturday
				1 Happy New Year	2	3
4 Winter	5	6 Shem 100	7	8	9	10
11	12	13	14	15	16	17
18	19	20	21	22	23	24
25	26	27	28	29		

Chart 71

Sunday	Monday	Tuesday	Wednesday	Thursday	Friday	Saturday
Arphaxad born Sunday February 17, 1658 GOWC *1984 Years BC						
*					1	2
3	4	5	6	7	8	9
10	11	12	13	14	15	16
17 Shem was 100 Arphaxad born	18	19	20	21	22	23
24	25	26	27	28	29	

And Shem lived after he begat Arphaxad five hundred years, and begat sons and daughters.   Genesis 11:11

Shem lived another 500 years after the birth of Arphaxad on February 17, exactly like Noah lived another 350 years after the Flood on February 17. God changed the seed of Adam birthday from January 6 to February 17 by saying after; –after– was established in the mouth of two or three witnesses proving doctrine.

Chart 72

Shem born Wednesday January 6, 1558 GOWC Shem died Tuesday February 17, 2158 GOWC and 1484 BC						
Sunday	Monday	Tuesday	Wednesday	Thursday	Friday	Saturday
					1 New Year	2
3	4 Winter	5	6	7	8	9
10	11	12	13	14	15	16
17th Arphaxad was born			17th Shem lived after Arphaxad born			
1, 8, 15, 22, 29, 36, 43, 50, 57, 64, 71, 78, 85, 92, 99, 106, 113, 120, 127, 134, 141, 148, 155, 162, 169, 176, 183, 190, 197, 204, 211, 218, 225, 232, 239, 246, 253, 260, 267, 274, 281, 288, 295, 302, 309, 316, 323, 330, 337, 344, 351, 358, 365, 372, 379, 386, 393, 400, 407, 414, 421, 428, 435, 442, 449, 456, 463, 470, 477, 484, 491, 498,						
Sunday	Monday	Tuesday	Wednesday	Thursday	Friday	Saturday
						499
		17th Shem lived 500 years				

Pay attention to the scripture's verses and the numerical order that Moses was narrating.

> And Arphaxad lived five and thirty years, and begat Salah: Arphaxad lived after he begat Salah four hundred and three years, and begat sons and daughters. Genesis 11:12, 13

Arphaxad 1658 birth years was added to Arphaxad 35 years lived equal Salah born Sunday February 17, 1693 GOWC. Arphaxad died Friday February 17, 2096 GOWC and 1546 BC.

> And Salah lived thirty years, and begat Eber: And Salah lived after he begat Eber four hundred and three years, and begat sons and daughters.
> Genesis 11:14, 15

Salah 1693 birth years was added to Salah 30 years lived equal Eber born Saturday February 17, 1723 GOWC. Salah died Thursday February 17, 2126 GOWC and 1516 BC.

> And Eber lived four and thirty years, and begat Peleg: And Eber lived after he begat Peleg four hundred and thirty years, and begat sons and daughters. Genesis 11:16, 17

Eber 1723 birth years was added to Eber 34 years lived equal Peleg born Wednesday February 17, 1757 GOWC. Eber died Friday February 17, 2187 GOWC and 1455 BC.

> And Peleg lived thirty years, and begat Reu: And Peleg lived after he begat Reu two hundred and nine years, and begat sons and daughters. Genesis 11:18, 19

Peleg 1757 birth years was added to Peleg 30 years lived equal Reu born Tuesday February 17, 1787 GOWC. Peleg died Saturday February 17, 1996 GOWC and 1646 BC.

> And Reu lived two and thirty years, and begat Serug: And Reu lived after he begat Serug two hundred and seven years, and begat sons and daughters. Genesis 11:20–21

Rue 1787 birth years was added to Reu 32 years lived equal Serug born Sunday February 17, 1819 GOWC. Reu died Friday February 17, 2026 GOWC and 1616 BC.

> And Serug lived thirty years, and begat Nahor: And Serug lived after he begat Nahor two hundred years, and begat sons and daughters. Genesis 11:22, 23

Serug 1819 birth years was added to Serug 30 years lived equal Nahor born Saturday February 17, 1849 GOWC. Serug died Thursday February 17, 2049 GOWC and 1593 BC.

> And Nahor lived nine and twenty years, and begat Terah: And Nahor lived after he begat Terah an hundred and nineteen years, and begat sons and daughters.   Genesis 11:24, 25

Nahor 1849 birth years was added to Nahor 29 years lived equal Terah born Tuesday February 17, 1878 GOWC. Nahor died Tuesday February 17, 1997 GOWC and 1645 BC.

And Terah lived seventy years, and begat Abram, Nahor, and Haran. And the days of Terah were two hundred and five years: and Terah died in Haran. Genesis 11:26, 32

Terah 1878 birth years was added to Terah 70 years lived equal Abram, Nahor, and Haran born Tuesday February 17, 1948 GOWC. Terah died Monday February 17, 2083 GOWC and 1559 BC.

Moses goes into more detail about the life of Abram.

Now the Lord had said unto Abram, Get thee out of thy country, and from thy kindred, and from thy father's house, unto a land that I will shew thee: and I will bless thee, and make thy name great; and thou shalt be a blessing: And I will bless them that bless thee, and curse him that curseth thee: and in thee shall all families of the earth be blessed. So Abram departed, as the Lord had spoken unto him; *and Lot went with him: and Abram was seventy and five years old when he departed out of Haran.* And Sarai Abram's wife took Hagar her maid the Egyptian, after Abram had dwelt ten years in the land of Canaan, and gave her to her husband Abram to be his wife. *And Abram was fourscore and six years old*, when Hagar bare Ishmael to Abram. Genesis 12:1–4, 16:3,16

Chart 73

Abram departed Wednesday February 17, 2023 GOWC						
Sunday	Monday	Tuesday	Wednesday	Thursday	Friday	Saturday
		17th Abram born			17th Abram lived	
43, 50, 57, 64, 71,						1, 8, 15, 22, 29, 36,
Sunday	Monday	Tuesday	Wednesday	Thursday	Friday	Saturday
	72			73		
74			17th Abram 75 departed			76
		77			78	
	79			80		
81			82			83
		84			85	
	86 Ishmael born			87		

And when Abram was ninety years old and nine, the Lord appeared to Abram, and said unto him, I am the Almighty God; walk before me, and be thou perfect. And Abraham was ninety years old and nine, when he was

69

circumcised in the flesh of his foreskin. And Ishmael his son was thirteen years old, when he was circumcised in the flesh of his foreskin. In the selfsame day was Abraham circumcised, and Ishmael his son. And all the men of his house, born in the house, and bought with money of the stranger, were circumcised with him. And Abraham was an hundred years old, when his son Isaac was born unto him. And the child grew, and was weaned: and Abraham made a great feast the same day that Isaac was weaned. And Sarah saw the son of Hagar the Egyptian, which she had born unto Abraham, mocking. And the thing was very grievous in Abraham's sight because of his son. And God said unto Abraham, Let it not be grievous in thy sight because of the lad, and because of thy bondwoman; And Abraham said unto his young men, Abide ye here with the ass; and the lad and I will go yonder and worship, and come again to you. *And these are the days of the ye ars of Abraham's life which he lived, an hundred threescore and fifteen years.* Then Abraham gave up the ghost, and died in a good old age, an old man, and full of years; and was gathered to his people. And his sons Isaac and Ishmael buried him in the cave of Machpelah, in the field of Ephron the son of Zohar the Hittie, which is before Mamre.   Genesis 17:1- 25:9

Moses gave us plenty of information about Abraham life, this information is incorporated in Chart 74.

Chart 74

Abram born Tuesday February 17, 1948 GOWC						
Abraham died Tuesday February 17, 2123 GOWC						
Sunday	Monday	Tuesday	Wednesday	Thursday	Friday	Saturday
		17th Abram born			17th Abraham lived circumcised	
					1, 8, 15, 22, 29, 36, 43, 50, 57, 64, 71, 78, 85, 92, 99,	
Sunday	Monday	Tuesday	Wednesday	Thursday	Friday	Saturday
	17th Abraham 100 Isaac born Ishmael 14 yrs.			17th Isaac 1 yr. Ishmael 15 yrs.		
17th Isaac 2 yrs. Ishmael 16 yrs.			17th Isaac 3 yrs. weaned Ishmael 17 yrs.			

Sunday	Monday	Tuesday	Wednesday	Thursday	Friday	Saturday
17th Abraham lived 116 yrs.			17th Abraham 117 yrs. offer Isaac 17 yrs. Ishmael 31 yrs.			17th Abraham lived after Isaac offer to God
						57, 50, 43, 36, 29, 22, 15, 8, 1
Sunday	Monday	Tuesday	Wednesday	Thursday	Friday	Saturday
		17th Abraham lived 58 yrs. died 175 years old				

Abram 1948 birth years was added to Abraham 175 years lived equal Abraham died Tuesday February 17, 2123 and 1519 BC.

You can check this for accuracy. Abraham death year 2123 minus Abram birth year 1948 equal 175 must be equally divisible by 7 equal 25.

> And these are the years of the life of Ishmael, an hundred and thirty and seven years: and he gave up the ghost and died; and was gathered unto his people. Genesis 25:17

Abraham 1948 birth years was added to Abraham 86 years lived equal Ishmael born Monday February 17, 2034 GOWC. Ishmael died Saturday February 17, 2171 GOWC and 1471 BC.

> And Isaac was forty years old when he took Rebekah to wife, the daughter of Bethuel the Syrian of Padanaram, the sister to Laban the Syrian. And Isaac intreated the Lord for his wife, because she was barren: and the Lord was intreated of him, and Rebekah his wife conceived. And the children struggled together within her; And when her days to be delivered were fulfilled, behold, there were twins in her womb. And the first came out red, all over like an hairy garment; and they called his name Esau. And after that came his brother out, and his hand took hold on Esau's heel; and his name was called Jacob: and Isaac was threescore years old when she bare them. And the days of Isaac were an hundred and fourscore years. And Isaac gave up the ghost, and died, and was gathered unto his people, being old and full of days: and his sons Esau and Jacob buried him. Genesis 25:20 – 35:29

Abraham 1948 birth years was added to Abraham 100 years lived equal Isaac born Monday February 17, 2048 GOWC. Isaac marries Rebekah

Tuesday February 17, 2088 GOWC. Esau and Jacob were born Saturday February 17, 2108 GOWC. Isaac died Tuesday February 17, 2228 GOWC and 1414 BC.

The scriptures allow you to solve problems. The birth of Joseph was in a word problem within his father Jacob's life.

> *And Joseph was thirty years old when he stood before Pharaoh king of Egypt.* And Joseph went out from the presence of Pharaoh, and went throughout all the land of Egypt. And in the seven plenteous years the earth brought forth by handfuls. *And he gathered up all the food of the seven years,* which were in the land of Egypt, and laid up the food in the cities: the food of the field, which was round about every city, laid he up in the same. *For these two years hath the famine been in the land*: and yet there are five years, in the which there shall neither be earing nor harvest. And Pharaoh said unto Jacob, How old art thou? *And Jacob said unto Pharaoh, he days of the years of my pilgrimage are an hundred and thirty years*: few and evil have the days of the years of my life been, and have not attained unto the days of the years of the life of my fathers in the days of their pilgrimage. *And Jacob lived in the land of Egypt seventeen years*: so the whole age of Jacob was an hundred forty and seven years. And the time drew nigh that Israel must die: and he called his son Joseph, and said unto him, If now I have found grace in thy sight, put, pray thee, thy hand under my thigh, and deal kindly and truly with me; bury me not, I pray thee, in Egypt: But I will lie with my fathers, and thou shalt carry me out of Egypt, and bury me in their burying place. And he said, I will do as thou hast said. And he said, Swear unto me. And he sware unto him. And Israel bowed himself upon the bed's head.
> Genesis 41:46 – 47:31 emphasis added

Joseph was 30 years old when he appears before Pharaoh. Add 7 years of plenteous and 2 years of famine, equals Joseph being 39 years old. Jacob was 130 years old when he appeared before Pharaoh minus Joseph's 39 years equals Jacob's age of 91 years lived when Joseph was born.

Jacob 2108 birth years was added to Jacob 91 years lived equal Joseph born Saturday February 17, 2199 GOWC. Jacob died Saturday February 17, 2255 GOWC and 1387 BC.

> So Joseph died, being an hundred and ten years old: and they embalmed him, and he was put in a coffin in Egypt.   Genesis 50:26

Joseph born Saturday February 17, 2199 GOWC. Joseph died Sunday February 17, 2309 GOWC and 1333 BC.

> And Joseph died, and all his brethren, and all that generation. And the children of Israel were fruitful, and increased abundantly, and multiplied, and waxed exceeding mighty; and the land was filled with them. Now there arose up a new king over Egypt, which knew not Joseph.   Exodus 1:6–8

Now, we will continue with Moses.

> Now the sojourning of the children of Israel, who dwelt in Egypt, was four hundred and thirty years. And it came to pass at the end of the four hundred and thirty years, even the selfsame day it came to pass, that all the hosts of the Lord went out from the land of Egypt.   Exodus 12:41, 42

And let add the apostle Paul for in the mouth of 2 or 3 witnesses.

> And this I say, that the covenant, that was confirmed before of God in Christ, the law, which was four hundred and thirty years after, cannot disannul, that it should make the promise of none effect.   Galatians 3:17

In the above scriptures contains 430 years. When Joseph died that was 71 years of Israel begin in the land of Egypt. 430 years minus 71 years equal 359 years remaining in the land of Egypt. So, you add Joseph death year 2309 GOWC plus 359 years remaining equal 2668 GOWC when Israel come out of Egypt in the fourth month.

Let us continue with Moses again.

> And the Lord spake unto Moses and Aaron in the land of Egypt saying, This month shall be unto you the beginning of months: it shall be the first month of the year to you. Speak ye unto all the congregation of Israel, saying, In the tenth day of this month they shall take to them every man a lamb, according to the house of their fathers, a lamb for an house: And ye shall keep it up until the fourteenth day of the same month: and the whole assembly of the congregation of Israel shall kill it in the evening.
> Genesis 12:1-3, 6

The Lord spoke unto Moses and Aaron on Saturday April/Abib 1, 2668 GOWC. They took the lamb on the tenth day and they killed the lamb on the fourteenth day. This is 973 Years 10 Months BC for the AEC Chart 75.

AEC Beginning

Chart 75

1st month April AEC 4th month April 2668 GOWC 973 Years 10 Months BC						
Sunday	Monday	Tuesday	Wednesday	Thursday	Friday	Saturday
						1 God speak to Moses
2	3	4	5 Spring	6	7	8
9	10	11	12	13	14 Passover	15 Left Egypt
16	17	18	19	20	21	22
23	24	25	26	27	28	29
30						

And Moses stripped Aaron of his garments, and put them upon Eleazar his son; and Aaron died there in the top of the mount: and Moses and Eleazar came down from the mount. And when all the congregation saw that Aaron was dead, they mourned for Aaron thirty days, even all the house of Israel. And Aaron the priest went up into mount Hor at the commandment of the LORD, and died there, in the fortieth year after the children of Israel were come out of the land of Egypt, in the first day of the fifth month. And Aaron was an hundred and twenty and three years old when he died in mount Hor. Numbers 20:28, 29 - 33:38, 39

Israel stops using GOWC on Saturday April 1, 2668 GOWC; four months before Aaron 84 birthday. So, Aaron was 83 years old plus Israel 40 years equal Aaron dying at the age of 123 in 40 AEC. This is the same process that Noah and Seth did after the Flood.

Aaron born Sunday August 1, 2751 GOWC. Aaron died Thursday August 1, 40 AEC and 933 Years 6 Months BC.

Aaron and John the Baptist shared the same birth date.

In which time Moses was born, and was exceeding fair, and nourished up in his father's house three months: And it came to pass in the fortieth year, in the eleventh month, on the first day of the month, that Moses spake unto the children of Israel, according unto all that the Lord had given him in commandment unto them; And the Lord spake unto Moses that selfsame day, saying, Get thee up into this mountain Abarim, unto mount Nebo, which is in the land of Moab, that is over against Jericho; and behold the land of

74

Canaan, which I give unto the children of Israel for a possession: And die in
the mount whither thou goest up, and be gathered unto thy people; as Aaron
thy brother died in mount Hor, and was gathered unto his people: And Moses
was hundred and twenty years old when he died.
Deuteronomy 1:3, 32:48–50, 34:7

Israel stops using GOWC Saturday April 1, 2668 GOWC; two months
after Moses' was 80 years old in GOWC. Then, Israel 40 years equal Moses
dying at the age of 120 in 40 AEC.

The Lord thy God will raise up unto thee a Prophet from the midst of thee,
of thy brethren, like unto me; unto him ye shall hearken.
Deuteronomy 18:15

Then those men, when they had seen the miracle that Jesus did, said, This is
of a truth that prophet that should come into the world.   John 6:14

Moses was born Saturday February 1, 2748 GOWC. Moses was cast into
the river on Wednesday May 1, 2664 GOWC. Moses died Sunday February
1, 40 AEC and 933 BC.

Moses was born on the Lord' day and he was cast into river on the day
the Lord was crucified and he died on the day the Lord was born.

After the death of Moses, the scripture said.

And the people came up out of Jordan on the tenth day of the first month,
and encamped in Gilgal, in the east border of Jericho.   Joshua 4:19

Joshua and Israel crossed over the Jordan river on Thursday April 10, 41
AEC.

King Jesus

And said unto him, Behold, thou art old, and thy sons walk not in thy ways:
now make us a king to judge us like all the nations. And Samuel told all the
words of the Lord unto the people that asked of him a king.
1 Samuel 8:5 – 10

When Jesus therefore perceived that they would come and take him by force,
to make him a king, he departed again into a mountain himself alone.
John 6:14, 15

Israel knew there were many nations that had kings. That means, there were probably even more fiscal calendars according to each nation beginning.

AUC Calendar Beginning

After the building of Rome (AUC) began Sunday March 1, 2888 years 2 months GOWC or Sunday March 1, 219 years 11 months AEC and now, all calendars are 753 Years 11 Months BC Chart 10.

This is where Jesus was born in zero BC could conclude because GOWC year and the AEC year plus St. Bede calendar year equal the birth years of Jesus Christ. But there is so much more, that if, Jesus was born in zero BC did not address it, it might remain undone. From the New Testament the apostle Paul fill in another time void.

> And after that he gave unto them judges about the space of four hundred and fifty year, until Samuel the prophet. And afterward they desired a king: and God gave unto them Saul the son of Cis, a man of the tribe of Benjamin, by the space of forty years.   Acts 13:20, 21

How do you determine when the judges ruled until the prophet Samuel, to king Saul? A course through the scriptures.

> David was thirty years old when he began to reign, and he reigned forty years. And he died in a good old age, full of days, riches, and honour:
> 2 Samuel 5:4, 1 Chronicles 29:28

This is using the scriptures as intended, a little here and a little there. King David reigned after king Saul, both reigned for 40 years, but we still need more scriptures to determine the calendar years for each, including the judge rules to the prophet Samuel.

> and Solomon his son reigned in his stead. Then Solomon began to build the house of the Lord at Jerusalem in mount Moriah, where the Lord appeared unto David his father, in the place that David had prepared in the threshing floor of Ornan the Jebusite. And he began to build in the second day of the second month, in the fourth year of his reign.
> 1 Chronicles 29:29 to 2 Chronicles 3:2

> And it came to pass in the four hundred and eightieth year after the children of Israel were come out of the land of Egypt, in the fourth year of Solomon's reign over Israel, in the month Zif, which is the second month, that he began

to build the house of the Lord. And the time that Solomon reigned in Jerusalem over all Israel was forty years.   1 King 6:1- 11:42

From the Introduction we know that this date is Sunday May/Zif 2, 480 AEC. King Solomon was in his 4th year reign that leaves 36 years more to reign. You add his remaining years to this calendar year 480 AEC equal 516 AEC and king Solomon reign ended. You subtract 40 years from 516 equal king Solomon reign beginning 476 AEC. King David reign ended 476 AEC and you subtract 40 years equal king David reign beginning 436 AEC. King David was born Sunday February 1, 406 AEC. Now, king Saul reign ended 436 AEC, you subtract 40 years, king Saul reign began in 396 AEC from the prophet Samuel. The 450 years until to the prophet Samuel is 450 years – 396 AEC years equal 54 years GOWC. Therefore, 2668 years GOWC minus 54 years GOWC = 2614 years GOWC. The judges ruled from 2614 GOWC to 396 AEC that's 450 years. Or 2614 GOWC plus 450 GOWC equal 3064 GOWC.

King Jesus and king David were both born on Sunday. Again, we could stop right here because no pundit can deny these truths.

After the reign of Solomon, you just add his son Rehoboam reign and continue add their son reign thereafter.

Rehoboam his son reigned in his stead and forty years old, and he reigned seventeen years [516 AEC to 533 AEC] in Jerusalem. Rehoboam slept with his father and Abijah his son reigned in his stead.
2 Chronicles 9:31-12:16 emphasis added

Now in the eighteenth year of king Jeroboam began Abijah to reign over Judah. He reigned three years [533 AEC to 536 AEC] in Jerusalem (King Jeroboam was Israel king).   2 Chronicles 13:1, 2 emphasis added

So Abijah slept with his fathers, and they buried him in the city of David: and Asa his son reigned in his stead. In his days the land was quiet ten years [536 AEC to 546 AEC]. And Asa slept with his fathers, and died in the one and fortieth year of his reign [577 AEC]. And Jehoshaphat his son reigned in his stead and strengthened himself against Israel.
2 Chronicles 14:1-17:1 emphasis added

And Jehoshaphat reigned over Judah: he was thirty and five years old when he began to reign, and he reigned twenty and five years [577 AEC to 602 AEC] in Jerusalem. And Jehoram his son reigned in his stead.
2 Chronicles 17:2-20:31 emphasis added

Anytime the scriptures said how old the king was when he began to reign you can determine his birthday from king David birthday. Jehoshaphat 577 minus 35 equal 542 AEC birth date minus king David 406 equal 136 from king David birthday. 136 divided by 7 equal 133 years on Sunday as king David birthday the remaining 3 years are Wednesday, Saturday, and finally Tuesday February 1, 542 AEC for Jehoshaphat birthday.

Jehoram was thirty and two years old when he began to reign, and he reigned eight years [602 AEC to 610 AEC] in Jerusalem.
2 Chronicles 21:1 emphasis added

So Ahaziah the son of Jehoram king of Judah reigned. Forty and two years old was Ahaziah when he began to reign, and he reigned one year [610 AEC to 611 AEC] in Jerusalem... But Athaliah the mother of Ahaziah saw that her son was dead, she...destroyed all the seed royal of the house of Judah. But Jehoshabeath, the daughter of the king, took Joash the son of Ahaziah, and stole him from among the king's sons that were slain, and put him and his nurse in a bedchamber. So Jehoshabeath, the daughter of king Jehoram, the wife of Jehoiada the priest [for she was the sister of Ahaziah], hid him from Athaliah, so that she slew him not. And he was with them hid in the house of God six years [611 AEC to 617 AEC]: and Athaliah reigned over the land. And all the people of the land rejoiced: and the city was quiet, after that they had slain Athaliah with the sword.
2 Chronicles 22:1-23:21 emphasis added

Joash was seven years old when he began to reign, and he reigned forty years [617 AEC to 657 AEC] in Jerusalem...And Amaziah his son reigned in his stead.   2 Chronicles 24:1, 27 emphasis added

Amaziah was twenty and five years old when he began to reign, and he reigned twenty and nine years [657 AEC to 686 AEC] in Jerusalem.
 2 Chronicles 25:1

Then all the people of Judah took Uzziah, who was sixteen years old, and made him king in the room of his father Amaziah... Sixteen years old was Uzziah when he began to reign, and he reigned fifty and two years [686 AEC to 738 AEC] in Jerusalem... Jotham his son reigned in his stead.
2 Chronicles 26:1, 3, 23 emphasis added

Jotham was twenty and five years old when he began to reign, and he reigned sixteen years in Jerusalem [738 AEC to 754 AEC]. His mother's name also was Jerushah, the daughter of Zadok And Jotham slept with his fathers, and they buried him in the city of David: and Ahaz his son reigned in his stead.
2 Chronicles 27:1-9 emphasis added

Ahaz was twenty years old when he began to reign, and he reigned sixteen years [754 AEC to 770 AEC] in Jerusalem: but he did not that which was right in the sight of the Lord, like David his father: And Ahaz slept with his fathers, and they buried him in the city, even in Jerusalem: but they brought him not into the sepulchres of the kings of Israel: and Hezekiah his son reigned in his stead.   2 Chronicles 28:1-9 emphasis added

Hezekiah began to reign when he was five and twenty years old, and he reigned nine and twenty years [770 AEC to 799 AEC] in Jerusalem. Manasseh his son reigned in his stead.
2 Chronicles 29:1-32:33 emphasis added

Manasseh was twelve years old when he began to reign, and he reigned fifty and five years [799 AEC to 854 AEC] in Jerusalem…Amon his son reigned in his stead.   2 Chronicles 33:1, 20 emphasis added

Amon was two and twenty years old when he began to reign, and reigned two years [854 AEC to 856 AEC] in Jerusalem…and the people of the land made Josiah his son king in his stead.
2 Chronicles 33:21, 25 emphasis added

Josiah was eight years old when he began to reign, and he reigned in Jerusalem one and thirty years [856 AEC to 887 AEC].   2 Chronicles 34:1

Israel Captivity and Release

Then the people of the land took Jehoahaz the son of Josiah, and made him king in his father's stead in Jerusalem. Jehoahaz was twenty and three years old when he began to reign, and he reigned three months [887 AEC to 887 AEC] in Jerusalem. And king of Egypt made Eliakim his brother king over Judah and Jerusalem, and turned his name to Jehoiakim. And Necho took Jehoahaz his brother, and carried him to Egypt.
2 Chronicles 36:1, 2, 4 emphasis added

Jehoiakim was twenty and five years old when he began to reign, and he reigned eleven years [887 AEC to 897 AEC] in Jerusalem…and Jehoiachin his son reigned in his stead.   2 Chronicles 36:5, 8 emphasis added

Jehoiachin was eight years old when he began to reign, and he reigned three month and ten days [897 AEC to 897 AEC] in Jerusalem. And when the year was expired, [898 AEC] king Nebuchadnezzar sent, and brought him to Babylon, with the goodly vessels of the house of the Lord, and made Zedekiah his brother king over Jerusalem. Zedekiah was one and twenty years old when he began to reign, and reigned eleven years [898 AEC to 909 AEC] in Jerusalem.   2 Chronicles 36:9-12 emphasis added

It came also in the days of Jehoiakim [887 AEC] the son of Josiah king of Judah, unto the end of the eleventh year of Zedekiah [909 AEC] the son of Josiah king of Judah, unto the carrying away of Jerusalem captive in the fifth month.   Jeremiah 1:1–3 emphasis added

In the first year of Darius the son of Ahasuerus, of the seed of the Medes, which was made king over the realm of the Chaldeans; In the first year of his reign I Daniel understood books the number of the years, whereof the word of the Lord came to Jeremiah the prophet, that he would accomplish seventy years in the desolations of Jerusalem.
Daniel 9:1–2 emphasis added

Now when the copy of king Artaxerxes' letter was read before Rehum, and Shimshai the scribe, and their companions, they went up in haste to Jerusalem unto the Jews, and made them to cease by force and power. Then ceased the work of the house of God which is at Jerusalem. So it ceased unto the second year (957 AEC) of the reign of Darius king of Persia.
Ezra 4:23–24 emphasis added

In the second year of Darius the king, in the sixth month, in the first day of the month (Monday September 1, 957 AEC), came the word of the Lord by Haggai the prophet unto Zerubbabel the son of Shealtiel, governor of Judah, and to Joshua the son of Josedech, the high priest, saying, Thus saith the Lord of hosts; Consider your ways. Go up to the mountain, and bring wood, and build the house; and I will take pleasure in it, and I will be glorified, saith the Lord…and they came and did work in the house of the Lord of hosts, their God, In the four and twentieth day of the sixth month in the second year of Darius the king (Wednesday September 24, 957 AEC).   Haggi 1:1-15

Temple of God Rebuilding

Chart 76

16 Years 5 Months BC 7th month September 737 AUC 6th month September 957 AEC 9th month September 3625 GOWC						
Sunday	Monday	Tuesday	Wednesday	Thursday	Friday	Saturday
	1	2	3	4	5	6
7	8	9	10	11	12	13
14	15	16	17	18	19	20
21	22	23	24	25	26	27
28	29					

The Temple of God completion is a direct connection to the ministry of Jesus Christ 46 years into the future Chart 33.

Chart 77

			16 Years 4 Months BC 8th month October 737 AUC 7th month October 957 AEC 10th month October 3625 GOWC			
Sunday	Monday	Tuesday	Wednesday	Thursday	Friday	Saturday
		1	2	3	4	5 Fall
6	7	8	9	10	11	12
13	14	15	16	17	18	19
20	21	22	23	24	25	26
27	28	29	30			

The voice of him that crieth in the wilderness, Prepare ye the way of the Lord, make straight in the desert a highway for our God.   Isaiah 40:3

Behold, I will send my messenger, and he shall prepare the way before me: Malachi 3:1

The voice of one crying in the wilderness, Prepare ye the way of the Lord, make his paths straight.   Mark 1:1–5

*Elisabeth Conception 15 Years BC

Chart 78

			16 Years 3 Months BC 9th month November 737 AUC 8th month November 957 AEC 11th month November 3625 GOWC			
Sunday	Monday	Tuesday	Wednesday	Thursday	Friday	Saturday
*				1	2	3
4	5	6	7	8	9	10
11	12	13	14	15	16	17
18	19	20	21	22	23	24
25	26	27	28	29		

Malachi and Isaiah go hand in hand with the ministry of John the Baptist beginning 46 years later from Chart 78 to Chart 32. And Elisabeth conceived John the Baptist 15 years later from Chart 78 to Chart 14.

God never left the world without His truth. From the first day, time never stopped, except once.

> Then spake Joshua to the Lord in the day when the Lord delivered up the Amorites before the children of Israel, and he said in the sight of Israel, Sun,

81

stand thou still upon Gibeon; and thou, Moon, in the valley of Ajalon. And the sun stood still, and the moon stayed, until the people had avenged themselves upon their enemies. **Is not this written in the book of Jasher?** So the sun stood still in the midst of heaven, and hasted not to go down about a whole day. And there was no day like that before it or after it, that the Lord hearkened unto the voice of a man: for the Lord fought for Israel. Joshua 10:12-14

When you read "about a whole day" that means 1 hour less than a day. And the book of Jasher do exist, alone with many others books not included in the 66 books of the Holy Bible. See how the scriptures constantly prove themselves in the mouth of 2 witnesses or 3 witnesses. If, the Holy Bible mention other books, than those books must agree with the Holy Bible. Here are 2 examples from the book of Jasher.

And it was in the fifty-six year of the life of Lamech when Adam died: nine hundred and thirty years old was he at his death: Jasher 3:14

And it came to pass after this that Joseph did in that year, the seventy-first year of the Israelites going down to Egypt.   Jasher 59:26

BIBLE STUDY

Adam, Seth, and Enos were all born on January 6 and they all died on Tuesday January 6. When you do the math for each death, Adam 930 GOWC, Seth 1042 GOWC, and Enos 1140 GOWC the math must equal an even number when divided by the 7 calendar years cycle.

1042 – 930 = 112 and 112 ÷ 7 = 16.
1140 – 930 = 210 and 210 ÷ 7 = 30.
1140 – 1042 = 98 and 98 ÷ 7 = 14.

Shem lived Tuesday January 6, 1658 GOWC this math must be true too, with Adam, Seth, and Enos death dates.

1658 – 930 = 728 and 728 ÷ 7 = 104.
1658 – 1042 = 616 and 616 ÷ 7 = 88.
1658 – 1140 = 518 and 518 ÷ 7 = 74.

When did Elijah goes into heaven?

So he died according to the word of the LORD which Elijah had spoken. And Jehoram reigned in his stead in the second year of Jehoram the son of Jehoshaphat king of Judah (603 AEC); because he had no son. And it came to pass, when the LORD would take up Elijah into heaven by a whirlwind, that Elijah went with Elisha from Gilgal.   2 Kings 1:17, 2:1

Elijah was taken up into heaven in the second year of Jehoram on Friday August 5, 603 AEC. Jesus Christ and Enoch were taken up into heaven on a Friday too.

How old was Isaac when Abraham offers him up to God?

And God said unto Abraham, Let it not be grievous in thy sight because of the lad, and because of thy bondwoman; And God heard the voice of the lad; and the angel of God called to Hagar out of heaven, and said unto her, And Abraham said unto his young men, Abide ye here with the ass; and I and the lad will go yonder and worship, and come again to you.
Genesis 21:12 – 22:5

These are the generations of Jacob. Joseph, being seventeen years old, was feeding the flock with his brethren; and the lad was with the sons of Bilhah, and with the sons of Zilpah, his father's wives: and Joseph brought unto his father their evil report. And Judah said unto Israel his father, Send the lad (Benjamin) with me, and we will arise and go; that we may live, and not die, both we, and thou, and also our little ones.   Genesis 37:2, 43:8

One of his disciples, Andrew, Simon Peter's brother, saith unto him. There is a lad here, which hath five barley loaves, and two small fishes: but what are they among so many?   John 6:9

Here is the key word "lad".   The scriptures called Joseph a lad of seventeen years old and Judah called his brother Benjamin a lad. God called Ishmael a lad. Abraham call Isaac a lad. When was Jesus Christ a lad? Tuesday February 1, AD 17 Chart 23.

The Pharisees question Jesus about this.

Thou bearest record of thyself; thy record is not true. I am one that bear witness of myself, and the Father that sent me beareth witness of me.
John 8:13-18

Even Jesus proved He wasn't alone. The trial of Jesus Christ was done through the witnesses of Matthew, Mark, Luke, and John in a calendar year. As you rightly divide the word of truth by chapters and verses, you can determine the order of events.

Wednesday April 14, AD 31

And as soon as it was day, the elders of the people and the chief priests and the scribes came together, and led him into their council, saying, Art thou the Christ? tell us.   Luke 22:66-67

And the chief priests and all the council sought for witness against Jesus to put him to death; and found none. For many bare false witnesses against him, but their witness agreed not together.   Mark 14:55, 56

Now the chief priests, and elders, and all the council, sought false witness against Jesus, to put him to death; But found none: yea, though many false witnesses came, yet found they none.   Matthew 26:59, 60

At the last came two false witnesses, And said, This fellow said, I am able to destroy the temple of God, and to build it in three days. Matthew 26:61

And there arose certain, and bare false witness against him, saying, We heard him say, I will destroy this temple that is made with hands, and within three days I will build another made without hands. But neither so did their witness agree together.   Mark 14:57-59

And the high priest arose, and said unto him, Answerest thou nothing? what is it which these witness against thee? But Jesus held his peace, Matthew 26:62

And the high priest stood up in the midst, and asked Jesus, saying, Answerest thou nothing? what is it which these witness against thee? But he held his peace, and answered nothing.   Mark 14:60

First, you must admit no false witness agree against Jesus Christ. Secondly, when Jesus held his peace, they could not condemn Him to death.

And he said unto them, If I tell you, ye will not believe: And if I also ask you, ye will not answer me, nor let me go.   Luke 22:67

Again, the high priest asked him, and said unto him, Art thou the Christ, the Son of the Blessed? And Jesus said, I am: and ye shall see the Son of man sitting on the right hand of power, and coming in the clouds of heaven. Mark 14:61, 62

And the high priest answered and said unto him, I adjure thee by the living God, that thou tell us whether thou be the Christ, the Son of God. Matthew 26:63

Jesus saith unto him, Thou hast said: nevertheless I say unto you, Hereafter shall ye see the Son of man sitting on the right hand of power, and coming in the clouds of heaven.   Matthew 26:64

Hereafter shall the Son of man sit on the right hand of the power of God. Then said they all, Art thou then the Son of God? And he said unto them, Ye say that I am.   Luke 22:69, 70

What need we any further witness? For we ourselves have heard of his own mouth.   Luke 22:71

Then the high priest rent his clothes, saying, He hath spoken blasphemy; what further need have we of witnesses? behold, now ye have heard his blasphemy. What think ye? They answered and said, He is guilty of death. Matthew 26:65, 66

Then the high priest rent his clothes, and saith, What need we any further witnesses? Ye have heard the blasphemy: what think ye? And they all condemned him to be guilty of death.   Mark 14:63, 64

Finally, only when Jesus Christ spoke the truth, did they condemn Him to death by saying, "For we ourselves heard Him." This gave them in the mouth of 2 or 3 witnesses. How many people have read those scriptures and did not realize that that was a doctrinal truth?

Is there 1 God or 3 God?

Hear, O Israel: The Lord our God is one Lord: Deuteronomy 6:4

And Jesus answered him, The first of all the commandments is, Hear, O Israel; The Lord our God is one Lord: Mark 12:29

And the scribe said unto him, Well, Master, thou hast said the truth: for there is one God; and there is none other but he: Mark 12:32

One Lord, one faith, one baptism,   Ephesians 4:5

My answer is one God.

Here is the doctrine of baptismal.

And, behold, thou shalt conceive in thy womb, and bring forth a son, and shalt call his name Jesus.   Luke 1:31

The name of the Son is Jesus.

The Son is speaking.

I am come in my Father's name, and ye receive me not: if another shall come in his own name, him ye will receive.   John 5:43

The name of the Father is Jesus.

The Son is speaking.

But the Comforter, which is the Holy Ghost, whom the Father will send in my name, he shall teach you all things, and bring all things to your remembrance, whatsoever I have said unto you.   John 14:26

The name of the Holy Ghost is Jesus
Friday April 30, AD 31

And Jesus came and spake unto them, saying, All power is given unto me in heaven and in earth. Go ye therefore, and teach all nations, **baptizing them in the name of the Father, and of the Son, and of the Holy Ghost:** Teaching them to observe all things whatsoever I have commanded you: and, lo, I am with you always, even unto the end of the world.
Matthew 28:18 – 20

Who teaching must we follow? Jesus Christ through the apostles. Many have been baptized wrong in the titles of the Father, and of Son, and of the Holy Ghost those titles are not a name. How did the apostles baptize?

Then Peter said unto them, Repent, and **be baptized every one of you in the name of Jesus Christ for** the remission of sins, and ye shall receive the gift of the Holy Ghost.   Acts 2:38

Know ye not, that so many of us as were **baptized into Jesus Christ** were baptized into his death?   Romans 6:3

Who, when they were come down, prayed for them, that they might receive the Holy Ghost: (For as yet he was fallen upon none of them: only they were **baptized in the name of the Lord Jesus.**)   Acts 8:15, 16

When they heard this, they were baptized in the name of the Lord Jesus.
Acts 19:5

You must be baptized in the name of Jesus Christ or the name of the Lord Jesus or you have not been baptized.

How many ways are there to God?

Wherefore God also hath highly exalted him, and given him a name which is above every name: That at the name of Jesus every knee should bow, of things in heaven, and things in earth, and things under the earth; And that every tongue should confess that Jesus Christ is Lord, to the glory of God the Father.   Philippians 2:9-11

Neither is there salvation in any other: for there is none other name under heaven given among men, whereby we must be saved. Now when they saw the boldness of Peter and John, and perceived that they were unlearned and ignorant men, they marvelled; and they took knowledge of them, that they had been with Jesus.   Acts 4:12, 13.

There is only 1 way to God, and Jesus is it!

Name your faith using the scriptures?

Speak unto all the congregation of the children of Israel, and say unto them, Ye shall be holy: for I the Lord your God am holy.   Leviticus 19:2

But ye, beloved, building up yourselves on your most holy faith, praying in the Holy Ghost,   Jude 1:20

My answer is holy.

Let's go to AD 53.

Chart 79

1st month February AD 53 11th month February 1026 AEC 2nd month February 3695 GOWC 12th month February 806 AUC						
Sunday	Monday	Tuesday	Wednesday	Thursday	Friday	Saturday
					1 Merry Christmas Happy New Year	2
3	4	5	6	7	8	9
10	11	12	13	14	15	16
17	18	19	20	21	22	23
24	25	26	27	28	29	

Chart 80

2nd month March AD 53 12th month March 1026 AEC 3rd month March 3695 GOWC 1st month March 807 AUC						
Sunday	Monday	Tuesday	Wednesday	Thursday	Friday	Saturday
						1 New Year
2	3	4	5	6	7	8
9	10	11	12	13	14 Purim	15 Purim
16	17	18	19	20	21	22
23	24	25	26	27	28	29

Did the apostle Paul change the Commandment Sabbath from Saturday to Sunday because of this scripture?

> Upon the first day of the week let every one of you lay by him in store, as God hath prospered him, that there be no gatherings when I come.
> 1 Corinthians 16:2

My answer would be no. Especially, when you consider the first day of the week is the first day of work. And then consider these scriptures.

> And Paul, as his manner was, went in unto them, and three sabbath days reasoned with them out of the scriptures, opening and alleging, that Christ must needs have suffered, and risen again from the dead; and that this Jesus, whom I preach unto you, is Christ.   Acts 17:2, 3 emphasis added

> Paul…And he reasoned in the synagogue every sabbath, and persuaded the Jews and the Greeks.   Acts 18:1 emphasis added

> And when Paul…And he went into the synagogue, and spake boldly for the space of three months, And this continued by the space of two years.
> Acts 19:6, 8, 10 emphasis added

When you dig further into that question, you will come across these scriptures.

> I knew a man in Christ above fourteen years ago, (whether in the body, I cannot tell; or whether out of the body, I cannot tell: God knoweth;) such an one caught up to the third heaven. And I knew such a man, (whether in the body, or out of the body, I cannot tell: God knoweth;) How that he was caught up into paradise, and heard unspeakable words, which it is not lawful for a man to utter.   2 Corinthians 12:1-4

The apostle Paul was describing the time he was stone, Acts chapter 14:19-20, and that was over 14 years. Let us add more scriptures to that.

> And we sailed away from Philippi after the days of unleavened bread, and came unto them to Troas in five days; where we abode seven days. And upon the first day of the week, when the disciples came together to break bread, Paul preached unto them, ready to depart on the morrow; and continued his speech until midnight. And there sat in a window a certain young man named Eutychus, being fallen into a deep sleep: and fell down from the third loft, and was taken up dead. And Paul went down, and fell on him, Trouble not yourselves; for his life is in him. When he therefore was come up again, and had broken bread, and eaten, and talked a long while, even till break of day,

so he departed...For Paul had determined to sail by Ephesus, for he hasted, if it were possible for him, to be at Jerusalem the day of Pentecost.
Acts 20:6–16 emphasis added

Now, between Acts 14:21 and Acts chapter 20:6-16 there were several more years afterward, which must be at least 7 years plus some months to bring you to at least 22 years. The apostle Paul became a Christian in AD 31 plus 22 years equal AD 53. If, the calendar year is right then the last scriptures above would be correspondingly correct within this calendar year Charts 79-83.

And ye shall count unto you from the morrow after the sabbath, from the day that ye brought the sheaf of the wave offering; seven sabbaths shall be complete: Even unto the morrow after the seventh sabbath shall ye number fifty days; and ye shall offer a new meat offering unto the Lord.
Leviticus 23:15-16

Pentecost is 50 days after feast of Unleavened bread sabbath on April 15. This also include counting 7 Commandment sabbaths before the 50 days.

Chart 81

3rd month April AD 53 1st month April 1027 AEC 4th month April 3695 GOWC 2nd month April 807 AUC						
Sunday	Monday	Tuesday	Wednesday	Thursday	Friday	Saturday
1 New Year	2	3	4	5 Spring	6	7
8	9	10 Lamb taken	11	12	13	14 Passover Sabbath
15 Paul at Philippi Unleavened Sabbath	16	17	18	19	20	21 1 Sabbath
22 Unleavened bread end	23 Paul leaves	24	25	26	27	28 2 Sabbath Paul in Troas
29	30					

90

Chart 82

			4th month May AD 53 2nd month May 1027 AEC 5th month May 3695 GOWC 3rd month May 807 AUC			
Sunday	Monday	Tuesday	Wednesday	Thursday	Friday	Saturday
		1	2	3	4	5 3 Sabbath Paul aboded 7 days
6 Paul raised young man	7 Paul leaves to Jerusalem	8	9	10	11	12 4 Sabbath
13	14 Second Passover	15	16	17	18	19 5 Sabbath
20	21	22	23	24	25	26 6 Sabbath
27	28	29				

Chart 83

			5th month June AD 53 3rd month June 1027 AEC 6th month 3695 GOWC 4th month 807 AUC			
Sunday	Monday	Tuesday	Wednesday	Thursday	Friday	Saturday
			1	2	3	4 7 Sabbath
5 49 days	6 50 days Pentecost	7	8	9	10	11
12	13	14	15	16	17	18
19	20	21	22	23	24	25
26	27	28	29	30		

The apostle Paul did not change the Commandment Sabbath to the first day of the week Sunday while still honoring the Commandment Sabbath 22 years later. This is just another lie of the devil.

Let's used the calendar for the next scriptures.

> Salute every saint in Christ Jesus. The brethren which are with me greet you. All the saints salute you, chiefly they that are of Caesar's household. The grace of our Lord Jesus Christ be with you all.   Philippians 4:21-23

The Wikipedia on-line encyclopedia, said Claudius Caesar was born August 1, 10 BC and died October 13, AD 54 at the age of 64. August 1, 10 BC went uncontested until now, because there was no way of verifying that date. Now, by using John the Baptist birth month and date, which was the same as Claudius Caesar, then count backward 9 years from Chart 23. Claudius Caesar was born Saturday August 1, 9 Years 6 Months BC. Claudius Caesar died Wednesday October 13, AD 54 at the age of 64 was right Chart 84.

Chart 84

9th month October AD 54						
Sunday	Monday	Tuesday	Wednesday	Thursday	Friday	Saturday
					1	2
3	4	5 Fall	6	7	8	9
10	11	12	13 Caesar died	14	15	16
17	18	19	20	21	22	23
24	25	26	27	28	29	30

How can any Wikipedia on-line encyclopedia BC year be right, if the reference did not know when Jesus Christ was born? However, if the calendar month and date are right along with the AD date, then you could determine the actual date as done with Claudius Caesar. Furthermore, Claudius Caesar was a Roman, his birth and death should have been recorded using the AUC calendar.

Claudius Caesar was born Saturday August 1, 744 AUC.

Claudius Caesar died Wednesday October 13, 808 AUC.

Converting the calendars is easy to do when you know their beginning.

Claudius Caesar was born Saturday August 1, 964 AEC.

Claudius Caesar died Wednesday October 13, 1028 AEC.

Claudius Caesar was born Saturday August 1, 3632 GOWC.

Claudius Caesar died Wednesday October 13, 3696 GOWC.

St. Bede died Monday May 26, AD 735 and Claudius Caesar died Wednesday October 13, AD 54 that's 681 years later. And AD 681 started on Saturday February 1. Remember, Jesus Christ turned 2 years old on Saturday February 1, AD 2 therefore, the math must agree. When you subtract 2 years from 681 equal 679 this must be divisible by 7 equal 97. So, AD 679 is Sunday February 1, the day Jesus Christ was born and AD 680 is Wednesday February 1, and AD 681 is Saturday February 1.

> Be ye therefore perfect, even as your Father which is in heaven is perfect.
> Matthew 5:48

92

Milton Keynes UK
Ingram Content Group UK Ltd.
UKHW042226180324
439698UK00005B/506